Voices from America's Past

The Westward Movement
1832-1889

Second Edition

Edited by Richard B. Morris
Gouverneur Morris Professor Emeritus of History
Columbia University
New York, New York

James Woodress
Professor of English
University of California
Davis, California

Webster Division, McGraw-Hill Book Company

New York • St. Louis • San Francisco • Dallas • Düsseldorf • Johannesburg
Kuala Lumpur • London • Mexico • Montreal • New Delhi • Panama • Paris
Rio de Janeiro • São Paulo • Singapore • Sydney • Tokyo • Toronto

Acknowledgments

11-13: By permission of Yale University Press, from *A Frontier Lady*, by Sarah Royce. 14-16: By permission of American Book Company, from *Washington Irving on the Prairie*, by Henry Ellsworth, edited by Williams and Simison. 17-19: By permission of The Wistar Institute of Anatomy and Biology, from *Autobiography of Isaac Jones Wistar*. 32-33: By permission of California Historical Society, from *California Historial Society Quarterly*, Vol. 28 (1949), p. 128. 40-41: By permission of Dodd, Mead & Co., from *Geronimo's Story of His Life*, S.M. Barrett, originally published by Duffield & Co., New York, 1906. 56-58: By permission of Harper & Brothers, from *Giants in the Earth*, by O.E. Rölvaag, Copyright 1927 by Harper & Brothers. 58-60: By permission of University of Nebraska Press from *The Kingdom of Art: Willa Cather's First Principles and Critical Statements, 1893-1896*, edited by Bernice Slote.

Library of Congress Cataloging in Publication Data on inside back cover

ISBN 0-07-043266-X

Second Edition Designed and Revised by
Educational Challenges, Incorporated, Washington, D.C.

Table of Contents

Voices From America's Past

This is one of a series of booklets containing the story of America as told by those who lived it, the participants and eyewitnesses. The selections included in this series are taken from the records that historians use in writing their books. These personal records, narratives, and public documents are the raw material of history. They bring us face to face with the people of the time and tell us something of their feelings, beliefs, and concerns as well as the events through which they lived. History books can expose to our view the framework of a country's development, but these firsthand reports put flesh on the bones of history.

In editing this booklet we have modernized punctuation, capitalization, and spelling when necessary to make the selections clear. Words added by the editors are enclosed in square brackets. Where we have made cuts, we have indicated them by spaced periods.

1607-1770 Beginnings of Colonial America
1770-1783 The Times That Tried Men's Souls
1783-1801 The Young Republic
1801-1829 The Jeffersonians
1829-1848 Jacksonian Democracy
1832-1889 The Westward Movement
1850-1865 A House Divided: The Civil War
1865-1914 The Shaping of an Industrial Nation
1867-1914 The United States as a New World Power
1914-1920 The First World War
1920-1939 Boom and Bust
1937-1946 The United States in World War II
1946-1961 Origins of the Cold War
1946-1962 From Truman to Kennedy
1962-1975 Years of National Turmoil
1962-1975 Hope and Anguish in Foreign Relations

Preface

It is hard to fix a beginning date for the westward movement, unless we start with Columbus' first voyage of discovery in 1492. In reality most of the history of the New World since then is the story of the movement of Europeans to the Western Hemisphere. It also is the story of the Indian peoples, who were pushed aside and overwhelmed by the Europeans, and, to a lesser extent, it is the story of Japanese and Chinese migrations to the United States.

Earlier booklets in this series have covered the expedition of Lewis and Clark to the Pacific Coast in 1805 and the annexation of Texas in 1845. This booklet is primarily concerned with the region beyond the Mississippi River—the high plains, the Rocky Mountains, the Sierra Nevada Mountains, the deserts, and the fertile Pacific Coast.

Restlessness and mobility have always been distinguishing characteristics of the American people. Revolutionary War veterans settled in Ohio or Kentucky and lived to see their children move on to Missouri or Texas. Their children's children pushed farther west to the Pacific Coast over the Oregon Trail or sailed around Cape Horn to join the gold rush in California. The westward movement still goes on, as a glance at the latest census report will quickly show. Nowadays, however, the immigrant can arrive in California in a few hours by jet from New York, pan gold on the assembly line of a company making guided missiles, and sleep in a ready-made cabin with modern conveniences.

This booklet begins with descriptions of the land and the people in the Great West before the Civil War. This was a period of exploration and conquest of the land. Until they saw for themselves, people could not believe the plains were as broad, the deserts as hot and dry, and the mountains as rugged and high as they really were. Every day was an adventure, some of which ended disastrously. But the West was conquered and the continent spanned by trail, by stagecoach route, and finally by railroad.

When one speaks of the frontier, it is important to keep

in mind that there was more than one frontier as the West filled up. There was, in the beginning, the frontier of the explorer and trapper. These first arrivals had no more effect on the land than the Indians who had roamed the mountains and plains for thousands of years. Next there was the mining frontier, which brought mushroom growth to specific areas like central California or Denver, Colorado, but left untouched the vast areas in between. Then there was the ranching frontier which created cow towns and cattle trails. Finally, there was the farming frontier, which changed the face of the land forever and filled the gaps left by the miners and ranchers.

The frontier of the trappers and explorers ended with the discoveries of gold and silver and the expansion of the borders of the United States all the way to the Pacific Coast. The frontier of the farmer ended when the entire West was more or less fenced in and dotted with settlements. The closing of the frontier was dramatically announced in 1890 by the director of the census, who reported that no longer could a line be drawn on the map showing the farthest point reached by settlements.

This booklet illustrates the various frontiers from the plains to the Pacific. The West has stimulated the American imagination as almost no other aspect of our history, and it would be impossible to list all the books, plays, movies, and television programs devoted to this subject. The firsthand reports of frontier days presented here are only a handful of the existing documents.

Richard B. Morris
James Woodress

A field gang at work in Illinois Library of Congress

1 The Land and the People

The Sierra Nevada Mountains

Col. John Frémont led several exploring expeditions into the Oregon Territory, mapped the Oregon Trail, and helped add California to the United States during the Mexican War. He later was one of California's first United States Senators and the first presidential candidate of the Republican Party. In 1844 we find him at the head of an expedition in the Sierra Nevada.

Col. John Frémont Describes His Expedition

In the account that follows, Frémont describes crossing the snowy range in February, over what is now Carson Pass, and descending along the approximate route of U.S. Highway 50 to Sacramento.

2d.—It had ceased snowing, and this morning the lower air was clear and frosty; and six or seven thousand feet above, the peaks of the Sierra now and then appeared among the rolling clouds, which were rapidly dispersing before the sun. Our Indian shook his head as he pointed to the icy pinnacles, shooting high up into the sky, and seeming almost immediately above us. Crossing the river on the ice, and leaving it immediately, we commenced the ascent of the mountain along the valley of a tributary stream. The people were unusually silent, for every man knew that our enterprise was hazardous, and the issue doubtful.

The snow deepened rapidly, and it soon became necessary to break a road. For this service, a party of ten was formed, mounted on the strongest horses, each man in succession opening the road on foot, or on horseback, until himself and his horse became fatigued, when he stepped aside, and, the remaining number passing ahead, he took his station in the rear. Leaving this stream, and pursuing a very direct course, we passed over an intervening ridge to the river we had left. . . .

The nut-pines were now giving way to heavy timber, and there were some immense pines on the bottom, around the roots of which the sun had melted away the snow; and here we made our camp and built huge fires. Today we had traveled 16 miles, and our elevation above the sea was 6,760 feet.

3d.—Turning our faces directly towards the main chain, we ascended an open hollow along a small tributary to the river which, according to the Indians, issues from a mountain to the south. The snow was so deep in the hollow that we were obliged to travel along the steep hillsides, and over spurs, where the wind and sun had in places lessened the snow, and where the grass, which appeared to be in good quality along the sides of the mountains, was exposed. We opened our road in the same way as yesterday, but made only seven miles, and encamped by some springs at the foot of a high and steep hill, by which the hollow ascended to another basin in the mountain. The little stream below was entirely buried in snow. . . .

4th—I went ahead early with two or three men, each with a lead horse to break the road. We were obliged to abandon the hollow entirely and work along the mountainside, which was very steep, and the snow covered with an icy crust. We cut a footing as we advanced and trampled a road through for the animals; but occasionally one plunged outside the trail, and slid along the field to the bottom, a hundred yards below. Late in the day we reached another bench in the hollow, where in summer the stream passed over a small precipice. Here was a short distance of dividing ground between the two ridges, and beyond an open basin, some ten miles across, whose bottom presented a field of snow. At the further or western side rose the middle crest of the mountain, a dark-looking ridge of volcanic rock.

The summit line presented a range of naked peaks, apparently destitute of snow and vegetation; but below, the face of the whole country was covered with timber of extraordinary size.

Towards a pass which the guide indicated here, we attempted in the afternoon to force a road; but after a laborious plunging through two or three hundred yards, our best horses gave out, entirely refusing to make any further effort, and, for the time, we were brought to a stand. The guide informed us that we were entering the deep snow, and here began the difficulties of the mountain; and to him, and almost to all, our enterprise seemed hopeless. . . .

5th—The night had been too cold to sleep, and we were up very early. Our guide was standing by the fire with all his finery on; and seeing him shiver in the cold, I threw on his shoulders one of my blankets. We missed him a few minutes afterwards, and never saw him again. He had deserted. . . .

6th—Accompanied by Mr. Fitzpatrick, I set out today with a reconnoitering [scouting] party on snowshoes. We marched all in single file, trampling the snow as heavily as we could. Crossing the open basin in a march of about ten miles, we reached the top of one of the peaks, to the left of the pass indicated by our guide. Far below us, dimmed by the distance, was a large snowless valley, bounded on the western side, at the distance of about a hundred miles, by a low range of mountains which [Kit] Carson recognized with delight as the mountains bordering the coast. "There," said he, "is the little mountain—it is fifteen years since I saw it; but I am just as sure as if I had seen it yesterday." Between us, then, and this low coast range, was the valley of the Sacramento.

Frémont and his companions retrace their steps to camp and spend the next four days preparing for the final ascent to the pass. The temperature dropped to three below zero on the eighth, and on the ninth snow fell. They now are camped at eight thousand feet.

11th—High wind continued, and our trail this morning was nearly invisible—here and there indicated by a little ridge of snow. Our situation became tiresome and dreary, requiring a strong exercise of patience and resolution.

In the evening I received a message from Mr. Fitzpatrick, acquainting me with the utter failure of his attempt to get our mules and horses over the snow—the half-hidden trail had proved entirely too slight to support them, and they had broken through, and were plunging about or lying half buried in snow. He was occupied in endeavoring to get them back to his camp; and in the meantime sent to me for further instructions. I wrote to him to send the animals immediately back to their old pastures; and, after having made mauls [heavy mallets] and shovels, turn in all the strength of his party to open and beat a road through the snow, strengthening it with branches and boughs of the pines.

12th—We made mauls, and worked hard at our end of the road all day. The wind was high, but the sun bright, and the snow thawing. We worked down the face of the hill, to meet the people at the other end. Towards sundown it began to grow cold, and we shouldered our mauls and trudged back to camp. . . .

14th—The dividing ridge of the Sierra is in sight from this encampment. . . .

16th—We had succeeded in getting our animals safely to the first grassy hill; and this morning I started with Jacob on a reconnoitering expedition beyond the mountain. We traveled along the crests of narrow ridges, extending down from the mountain in the direction of the valley, from which the snow was fast melting away. On the open spots was tolerably good grass; and I judged we should succeed in getting the camp down by way of these. Towards sundown we discovered some icy spots in a deep hollow; and, descending the mountain, we encamped on the headwater of a little creek, where at last the water found its way to the Pacific. . . .

I was now perfectly satisfied that we had struck the stream on which Mr. [John] Sutter lived; and turning about, made a hard push, and reached the camp at dark. Here we had the pleasure to find all the remaining animals, 57 in number, safely arrived at the grassy hill near the camp. . . .

On the 19th, the people were occupied in making a road and bringing up the baggage; and, on the afternoon of the next day, *February 20, 1844,* we encamped, with the animals and all the *matériel* of the camp, on the summit of the PASS [Carson Pass, altitude, 8,635 ft.] in the dividing ridge.

The expedition then began the descent towards the Sacramento River Valley, which was just as hard as the climb. By the time they reached lower altitudes, where they found grass for their horses and mules and game and fish for themselves, they were nearly exhausted and their animals almost starved. But the journey ended safely, and the party reached Sutter's ranch on the American River on March 6.

Why might explorers want to face the challenge of the wilderness? Would you have wanted to be part of an expedition like Frémont's? Why or why not?

The Desert Barrier

It is hard today to realize the terrors that the desert held for settlers who toiled across the empty wastes by covered wagon in 1849. The trip, which now takes only a few hours by car, then required days of courage and endurance, plus careful preparation.

Sarah Royce Describes Crossing the Desert

In the following narrative Sarah Royce, whose son became the philosopher Josiah Royce, tells of her experiences in crossing the desert from Salt Lake City to the California gold fields. She was traveling in a single wagon with her two-year-old daughter, her husband, and several other men when the party lost its way. They had started before daylight and missed a turn which led to a grassy meadow and water. They found themselves at noon far out on the desert, short of water and of food for the oxen.

We began to look anxiously for the depression in the ground, and the holes dug, which we were told would mark the Sink of the Humboldt. But it was nearly noonday before we came to them. There was still some passable water in the holes, but not fit to drink clear, so we contrived to gather enough sticks of sage to boil some, made a little coffee, ate our lunch and, thus refreshed, we hastened to find the forking road. Our director had told us that within about two or three miles beyond the Sink we might look for the road, to the left, and we did look, and kept looking, and going on, drearily, till the sun got lower and lower, and night was fast approaching. Then the conviction, which had long been gaining ground in my mind, took possession of the whole party. We had passed the forks of the road before daylight, that morning, and were now miles out on the desert without a mouthful of food for the cattle and only two or three quarts of water in a little cask.

What could be done? Halt we must, for the oxen were nearly worn out and night was coming on. The animals must at least rest, if they could not be fed: and, that they might rest, they were chained securely to the wagon, for, hungry and thirsty as they were, they would, if loose, start off frantically in search of water and food, and soon drop down exhausted. Having fastened them in such a way that they could lie down, we took a few mouthfuls of food, and then, we in our wagon and the men not far off upon the sand, fell wearily to sleep; a forlorn little company wrecked upon the desert.

The first question in the morning was, "How can the oxen be kept from starving?" A happy thought occurred. We had, thus far on our journey, managed to keep something in the shape of a bed to sleep on. It was a mattress-tick, and, just before leaving Salt Lake, we had put into it some fresh hay—not very much, for our load must be as light as possible; but the old gentleman traveling with us also had a small straw mattress; the two together might keep the poor things from starving for a few hours. At once a small portion was dealt out to them and for the present they were saved. For ourselves we had food which we believed would about last us till we reached

A family crossing the desert — Library of Congress

the Gold Mines if we could go right on: if we were much delayed anywhere, it was doubtful. The two or three quarts of water in our little cask would last only a few hours, to give moderate drinks to each of the party.

They decide that they must return; the distance to the next waterhole is too far. Soon after they begin retracing their steps, they meet another group of emigrants who confirm their suspicions that they missed the turn fifteen miles back.

I had now become so impressed with the danger of the cattle giving out that I refused to ride except for occasional brief rests. So, soon after losing sight of the dust of the envied little caravan, I left the wagon and walked the remainder of the day. For a good while I kept near the wagon but, by and by, being very weary I fell behind. The sun had set before we reached the Sink, and the light was fading fast when the wagon disappeared from my sight behind a slight elevation; and, as the others had gone on in advance some time before, I was all alone on the barren waste. However, as I recognized the features of the neighborhood, and knew we were quite near the Sink, I felt no particular apprehension, only a feeling that it was a weird and dreary scene and instinctively urged forward my lagging footsteps in hopes of regaining sight of the wagon. . . .

The next morning we resumed our backward march after feeding out the last mouthful of fodder. The water in the little cask was nearly used up in making coffee for supper and breakfast; but, if only each one would be moderate in taking a share when thirst impelled him, we might yet reach the wells before any one suffered seriously. We had lately had but few chances for cooking; and only a little boiled rice with dried fruit, and a few bits of biscuit remained after we had done breakfast. If we could only reach the meadows by noon. But that we could hardly hope for, the animals were so weak and tired. There was no alternative, however, the only thing to be done was to go steadily on, determined to do and endure. . . .

I found no difficulty this morning in keeping up with the team. They went so slowly, and I was so preternaturally [unnaturally] stimulated by anxiety to get forward, that before I was aware of it I would be some rods ahead of the cattle, straining my gaze as if expecting to see a land of promise, long before I had any rational hope of the kind. My imagination acted intensely. I seemed to see Hagar, in the wilderness walking wearily away from her fainting child among the dried-up bushes, and seating herself in the hot sand. I seemed to become Hagar myself, and when my little one, from the wagon behind me, called out, "Mamma I want a drink"—I stopped, gave her some, noted that there were but a few swallows left, then mechanically pressed onward again, alone, repeating, over and over, the words, "Let me not see the death of the child."

Just in the heat of noonday we came to where the sage bushes were nearer together; and a fire, left by campers or Indians, had spread for some distance, leaving beds of ashes, and occasionally charred skeletons of bushes to make the scene more dreary. . . .

Wearily passed the hottest noonday hour, with many an anxious look at the horned-heads, which seemed to me to bow lower and lower, while the poor tired hoofs almost refused to move. The two young men had been out of sight for some time; when, all at once, we heard a shout, and saw a few hundred yards in advance a couple of hats thrown into the air and four hands waving triumphantly. As soon as we got near enough, we heard them call out, "Grass and water! Grass and water!" and shortly we were at the meadows.

Why does Sarah Royce express more concern for the oxen than she does for her hungry family? Why were single families traveling through such forbidding territory? What was the greatest threat to them?

The Prairies

When wagon trains reached Independence, Missouri, and prepared to set off for the Far West, they faced some six hundred miles of prairie before reaching the mountains. There was water, grass, and game (especially buffalo) in abundance, but it was an awesome spectacle to travel week after week across the empty plains. When Washington Irving, the writer, returned from many years in Europe, he wanted to see the prairie and joined an expedition in 1832 which traveled as far west as the present site of Oklahoma City. One of his companions was

Henry Ellsworth, a commissioner appointed by Andrew Jackson to inspect the lands in present-day Oklahoma.

Henry Ellsworth Accompanies Washington Irving Across the Plains

In the selection that follows, Ellsworth describes the prairie, tells how one of his company captured a wild horse, and recounts his own experience in shooting a buffalo.

The country today is truly delightful. The prairies are smooth, the streams frequent, and meandering [winding] so as to present a vigorous growth of stately trees on every side. The flowers of spring have disappeared and left the numerous stalks covered with seeds as mementoes of vernal [springlike] fragrance, but the autumnal blossoms mixed with the prairie grass never fail to attract the eye with delight, or refresh the lungs by their sweet odors. My late travelling companion, Dr. O'Dwyer, says Eden was here and not on the Euphrates: "Adam's paradise was in these prairies!"

Mr. Irving said often today that the most splendid parks in England did not surpass the beautiful scenery around us, and yet between both there was such a striking resemblance as to recall to his mind at once the delightful rambles he had in Europe where art had been lavish in her favors to enhance the beauties of nature. I can say also, though my residence in Europe was short, that I beheld no scenery there so truly beautiful and grand as the rich prairies of the West. And if the prairies now are so charming, what must they be decked with the variegated plumage of spring? . . .

I ought perhaps to mention [that] the woods on these parks afforded [provided] excellent varieties of fruits. The season now was too late for most of them—the persimmon, haws, and winter grape were very abundant.

Our ride was made more cheering by the fresh signs of buffalo. Not the short grass but tracks and recent dung (resembling entirely that of our oxen and cows) assured us we should soon meet these *terrific* animals. Excavations in the ground showed where they indulged in their great pastime, in *wallowing*. The excavations are generally about 10 feet in diameter and 12 to 20 inches deep. It is these hollows, especially when filled with water, that make the chase, as I found it afterwards, so difficult and dangerous. The trees also furnish *their* evidence and every low limb was worn by the buffalo while scratching his skin after coming out of his mud or sand bath.

As soon as we had arrived at camp this evening, Billet requested the privilege to hunt a while, and mounting his horse with lariat [lasso] and gun, cantered off, and was

Western pioneers breaking the land

Library of Congress

soon out of sight. The firing on all sides assured us we should have plenty of game, and the hunters soon returned loaded with deer, turkeys, etc. It was not until after supper that Billet came to our camp quite out of breath and asked for help to bring in a wild horse he had just caught the other side of Red Fork. He had brought him through the river, but got him no farther. . . .

The horse was soon brought in, trembling at the sight of so many new things. He was between two and three years old, well made, and will doubtless make an excellent horse. The horse struggled for a while against Billet's mode of civilization and fell exhausted in the struggle. He panted and lay as submissive as a lamb. Twenty or thirty handled him from head to foot without any offer on his part to make resistance. He gave up the contest and submitted unconditionally and never afterwards was more disobedient than colts in general, nor indeed as much. . . . Tomorrow Billet said he should pack him with a saddle and make him do his share of work. We did not believe it possible and waited with curiosity to see the experiment. [He succeeded.]

Billet is an adventuresome as well as brave man. He has had both arms and one leg broken during exploits besides having his ribs on one side mashed in. He told us when he saw the horses they were distant from him. He stopped, laid down his gun, adjusted his saddle, and with lariat in hand he put spurs to his race horse, whose speed I never saw excelled. The wild horses stood amazed for a moment, then started and fled. They ran up a small hill and descending again were for a moment out of sight. When Billet came to the brow, he was frightened: a precipice was before him which he must leap or lose his prize. He chose the former, shut his eyes, and strained upon the reins and safely landed upon the bottom—a leap of 25 feet. His horse, accustomed to the race, soon recovered from the shock and continued pursuit. The race now continued for 1½ miles. He then reached the horses, and having failed in his first effort to take a Pawnee mare (with a slit in her ears) he put his lariat over the head of the horse brought to the camp. It was truly a great exploit. . . .

No sooner had I reined my horse towards the buffalo (notwithstanding he had been racing several hours and was then wet with perspiration) than he pricked up his ears and entered into a full run. I *never* went *half so fast before or mean to again*. I ran a quarter of a mile before [the] buffalo apprehended danger. They then began to make the best of their way to the west. Billet called out: "Remember the holes; let *him run;* let *him run.*" After running 1½ miles with gun in hand, almost tired to death and shook not a little, I came along side of the animal I had selected. He appeared a monster, for his weight was 1600. I fired. Billet said: "Take care; he will be upon you." The animal now began to throw blood from his mouth and nose, which satisfied me I had reached his heart. He stopped. I fired again. Both balls entered just *back of his fore shoulder.* He now came towards me with his tongue extended and his round full eye darting vengeance. My horse parried his movements, and I fired my rifle pistol and then seized the remaining one. At this moment the buffalo fell, exhausted with the loss of blood, and stretching out his legs died before I could get to him. . . . Billet performed the operation of cutting out his tongue, by opening the flesh on the under jaw and through this aperture taking the tongue, which I tied to my saddle and reached the camp a little after sunset.

From what viewpoint is Ellsworth evaluating the land? If he had thought about becoming a settler, how might he have viewed it differently? Compare the preparations needed for crossing the mountains, the desert, the prairies.

The Trappers

The fur trade was an important industry long before the Revolution, and by the time the westward movement opened up the region beyond the Mississippi, the fur trade had begun to decline. As the settlers moved west, the trappers moved farther west or gave up trapping and became scouts. Much of the West was first visited by the trappers, who ranged widely in their lonely and often hazardous work.

Isaac Jones Wistar Endures a Hard Winter

In the following selection we have printed an episode from the early career of Isaac Jones Wistar, who later became a general in the Union Army during the Civil War. Wistar at this time was running his trap lines in the Peace River region of western Canada. François is his partner. It is winter and they are trapping martens.

After the trapper has laid in his provisions, disposed of his horses, and settled down in his solitary winter quarters, incidents are few; and as none of a pleasant character are likely to occur, the fewer they are, the better for him. . . .

In our case about this time, martens being scarce and the camp, in consequence of the lateness of our arrival, having been badly chosen, it was found necessary to shift it in the dead of winter; for which purpose, taking but little provision from our scanty store and *caching* [hiding] the rest of our effects, we pushed out in a northerly direction, hoping to find a better location on some of the other tributaries of the Peace. But with ground covered by heavy snow, streams hard bound with ice, and frequent wind storms which at the low prevailing temperatures none can face and live, our progress was slow and no place looked very attractive. Hence no great time had elapsed before we found our provisions exhausted, in a difficult country with game not to be had. Making a temporary shelter in a bad place and under unfavorable circumstances, we therefore proceeded to devote our whole attention to hunting, till after some days we became awake to the fact that the district was absolutely without game. Every day the weather permitted, we covered long distances in opposite directions, without finding so much as a recent sign or track. Then we set traps for fish in such rapids as remained open, and for birds and small animals, but without success. . . .

After trying in vain all the resources practiced by trappers in such straits [difficult situations], all of which were well known to François, we ate the grease in our rifle stocks, all the fringes and unnecessary parts of our buckleather clothes, gun and ammunition bags, and every scrap of eatable material, boiling it down in an Assinaboine [Indian] basket with hot stones, and were finally reduced to buds and twigs. After many days of this extreme privation, no longer possessing strength to travel or hunt, I became discouraged; and as we lay down one night I determined to abandon the struggle and remain there, enduring with such fortitude as I might the final pangs, which could not be long deferred.

At this last stage in the struggle, an event occurred of the most extraordinary character, which cannot seem more strange and incredible to any one than it has always appeared to me on the innumerable occasions when I have since reflected on it. Notwithstanding our exhaustion and desperate conclusion of the night before. François rose at daylight, made up the fire as well as his strength permitted, blazed a tree near by on which he marked with charcoal a large cross, and carefully reloading and standing his gun against that emblem, proceeded to repeat in such feeble whispers as he was yet capable of, all the scraps of French and Latin prayers he could remember, to all of which I was in no condition to give much attention. When he got through he remarked with much cheerfulness that he was now sure of killing something and urged me to make one more effort with him, which I rather angrily refused, and bade him lie and and take what had to come, like a man. With cheerful assurance he replied that he was not afraid to die, but our time had not come. He knew he would find and kill, and we would escape all right.

Then desisting from his useless effort to get me up, François, leaving his heavy snow-shoes behind, directed himself with weak and uneven steps down the little stream in the deep gorge of which our camp was made; and never expecting to see him again, my mind relapsed into an idle, vacuous condition, in which external circumstances were forgotten or disregarded. But scarcely a few minutes had elapsed, and as it afterwards appeared he had hardly traversed a couple of hundred yards when I heard his gun, which I knew never cracked in vain.

I had thought myself unable to rise, but at that joyful sound promptly discovered my mistake. I found François in the spot from which he had fired, leaning against a tree in such deep excitement that he could speak with difficulty. On that rugged side hill apparently destitute [empty] of life, in that most improbable of all places, within sound and smell of our camp, he had seen, not a squirrel or a rabbit, but a deer. Attempting to climb for a better shot, the deer jumped, and with terrible misgivings he had fired at it running. He had heard it running after his shot but was sure he had made a killing hit. Scrambling with difficulty up the hill, we found a large clot of blood and a morsel of "lights" [lungs], which we divided and ate on the spot. After taking up the trail we soon found the animal. . . .

After passing safely through that period of starvation, we were glad enough to get back to the old camp and make the best of it during the remainder of the season, which furnished little more of incident to vary the monotony of our solitary occupation.

Why was trapping an important occupation on the frontier? Who bought furs? What for? What animals today are most valued for their skins? Where do furs come from today?

The Indians

When white settlers began moving across the prairies towards the Pacific coast, they encountered many different tribes of Indians who lived on the high plains. The Indians lived a nomadic life as they followed the buffalo herds from place to place. Eventually the tide of emigrants became a flood, the buffalo herds were destroyed, and the Indians were pushed off their traditional hunting grounds. Although the Indians fought to keep their land, they were hopelessly outnumbered.

Francis Parkman Visits an Indian Village

One of the best descriptions of Indian life before the Old West disappeared was written by Francis Parkman, the greatest American historian of the nineteenth century. As a youth, in 1846, Parkman traveled as far west as Wyoming for the purpose of studying the Indian character. In the following selection from his book, *The Oregon Trail,* he is reporting a visit to a village of the Sioux, also called the Dakotas.

At last the day drew to a close; and as the sun went down, the horses came trooping from the surrounding plains to be picketed before the dwellings of their respective masters. Soon within the great circle of lodges appeared another concentric circle of restless horses; and here and there fires glowed and flickered amid the gloom, on the dusky figures around them. I went over and sat by the lodge of Reynal. The Eagle-Feather, who was a son of Mene-Seela, and brother of my host the Big Crow, was seated there already, and I asked him if the village would move in the morning. He shook his head, and said that nobody could tell, for since old Mahto-Tatonka had died, the people had been like children that did not know their own minds. They were no better than a body without a head. So I, as well as the Indians themselves, fell asleep that night without knowing whether we should set out in the morning towards the country of the Snakes [the neighboring Indians].

At daybreak, however, as I was coming up from the river after my morning's ablutions [washing], I saw that a movement was contemplated. Some of the lodges were reduced to nothing but bare skeletons of poles; the leather covering of others was flapping in the wind as the squaws pulled it off. One or two chiefs of note had resolved, it seemed, on moving; and so having set their squaws at work, the example was followed by the rest of the village. One by one the lodges were sinking down in rapid succession, and where the great circle of the village had been only a few moments before, nothing now remained but a ring of horses and Indians, crowded in confusion together. The ruins of the lodges were spread over the ground, together with kettles, stone mallets, great ladles of horn, buffalo-robes, and cases of painted hide, filled with dried meat. Squaws bustled about in busy preparation, the old hags screaming to one another at the stretch of their leathern lungs. The shaggy horses were patiently standing while the lodge-poles were lashed to their sides, and the baggage piled upon their backs. The dogs, with tongues lolling out, lay lazily panting, and waiting for the time of departure. Each warrior sat on the ground by the decaying embers of his fire, unmoved amid the confusion, holding in his hand the long trail-rope of his horse.

As their preparations were completed, each family moved off the ground. The crowd was rapidly melting away. I could see them crossing the river, and passing in quick succession along the profile of the hill on the farther side. When all were gone, I mounted and set out after them, followed by Raymond, and, as we gained the summit, the whole village came in view at once, straggling away for a mile or more over the barren plains before us. Everywhere glittered the iron points of lances. The sun never shone upon a more strange array. Here were the heavy-laden pack-horses, some wretched old woman leading them, and two or three children clinging to their backs. Here were mules or ponies covered from head to tail with gaudy trappings, and mounted by some gay young squaw, grinning bashfulness and pleasure as the Meneaska [the white narrator] looked at her. Boys with miniature bows and arrows wandered over the plains, little naked children ran along on foot, and numberless dogs scampered among the feet of the horses. The young braves, gaudy with paint and feathers, rode in groups among the crowd, often galloping, two or three at once along the line, to try the speed of their horses. Here and there you might see a rank of sturdy pedestrians stalking along in their white buffalo-robes. These were the dignitaries of the village, the old men and warriors, to whose age and experience that wandering democracy yielded a silent deference. With the rough prairie and the broken hills for its background, the restless scene was striking and picturesque beyond description. Days and weeks made me familiar with it, but never impaired its effect upon my fancy.

As we moved on, the broken column grew yet more scattered and disorderly, until, as we approached the foot of a hill, I saw the old men before mentioned seating themselves in a line upon the ground, in advance of the whole. They lighted a pipe and sat smoking, laughing, and telling stories, while the people, stopping as they successively came up, were soon gathered in a crowd behind them. Then the old men rose, drew their buffalo-robes over their shoulders, and strode on as before. Gaining the top of the hill, we found a steep declivity [slope] before us. There was not a minute's pause. The whole descended in a mass, amid dust and confusion. The horses braced their feet as they slid down, women and children screamed, dogs yelped as they were trodden upon, while stones and earth went rolling to the bottom. In a few moments I could see the village from the summit, spreading again far and wide over the plain below.

What is most interesting to you about this description? Why? How does Parkman's picture of these Indians compare with the picture usually presented in stories and films?

The Emigrants

The Oregon Trail was a well-traveled route when Parkman visited Wyoming in 1846. Already many emigrants in covered wagons were moving westward from the Missouri River at Independence or Saint Joseph, then along the Platte River towards Wyoming and the South Pass over the Rockies.

Francis Parkman Meets a Wagon Train

In the next selection Parkman describes an emigrant party he encountered near the point where the trail struck the Platte River in central Nebraska.

About dark a sallow-faced fellow descended the hill on horseback, and splashing through the pool, rode up to the tents. He was enveloped in a huge cloak, and his broad felt hat was weeping about his ears with the drizzling moisture of the evening. Another followed, a stout, square-built, intelligent-looking man, who announced himself as leader of an emigrant party, encamped a mile in advance of us. About twenty wagons, he said, were with him; the rest of his party were on the other side of the Big Blue, waiting for a woman who was in the pains of childbirth, and quarreling meanwhile among themselves.

These were the first emigrants that we had overtaken, although we had found abundant and melancholy traces of their progress throughout the course of the journey. Sometimes we passed the grave of one who had sickened and died on the way. The earth was usually torn up, and covered thickly with wolf-tracks. Some had escaped this violation. One morning, a piece of plank, standing upright on the summit of a grassy hill, attracted our notice, and riding up to it, we found the following words very roughly traced upon it, apparently with a red-hot piece of iron:—

MARY ELLIS

DIED MAY 7TH, 1845

Aged two months.

Such tokens were of common occurrence.

We were late in breaking up our camp on the following morning, and scarcely had we ridden a mile when we saw . . . the emigrant caravan, with its heavy white wagons creeping on in slow procession, and a large drove of cattle following behind. Half a dozen yellow-visaged [faced] Missourians, mounted on horseback, were cursing and shouting among them, their lank angular proportions enveloped in brown homespun, evidently cut and adjusted by the hands of a domestic female tailor. As we approached, they called out to us: "How are ye, boys? Are ye for Oregon or California?"

Emigrants in camp

Library of Congress

As we pushed rapidly by the wagons, children's faces were thrust out from the white coverings to look at us; while the care-worn, thin-featured matron, or the buxom girl, seated in front, suspended the knitting on which most of them were engaged to stare at us with wondering curiosity. By the side of each wagon stalked the proprietor, urging on his patient oxen, who shouldered heavily along, inch by inch, on their interminable journey. It was easy to see that fear and dissension [disagreement] prevailed among them. . . . Many were murmuring against the leader they had chosen, and wished to depose him. . . .

We soon left them far behind, and hoped that we had taken a final leave; but our companions' wagon stuck so long in a deep muddy ditch, that before it was extricated the van [forefront] of the emigrant caravan appeared again, descending a ridge close at hand. Wagon after wagon plunged through the mud; and as it was nearly noon, and the place promised shade and water, we saw with satisfaction that they were resolved to encamp. Soon the wagons were wheeled into a circle: the cattle were grazing over the meadow, and the men, with sour, sullen faces, were looking about for wood and water. They seemed to meet but indifferent success. As we left the ground, I saw a tall slouching fellow . . . contemplating the contents of his tin cup, which he had just filled with water.

"Look here, you," said he; "it's chock-full of animals!"

The cup, as he held it out, exhibited in fact an extraordinary variety and profusion of animal and vegetable life.

Riding up the little hill, and looking back on the meadow, we could easily see that all was not right in the camp of the emigrants. The men were crowded together, and an angry discussion seemed to be going forward. R—— [one of Parkman's party] was missing from his wonted [usual] place in the line, and the Captain told us that he had remained behind to get his horse shod by a blacksmith attached to the emigrant party. Something whispered in our ears that mischief was on foot; we kept on, however, and coming soon to a stream of tolerable water, we stopped to rest and dine. Still the absentee lingered behind. At last, at the distance of a mile, he and his horse suddenly appeared, sharply defined against the sky on the summit of a hill; and close behind, a huge white object rose slowly into view.

"What is that blockhead bringing with him now?"

A moment dispelled the mystery. Slowly and solemnly, one behind the other, four long trains of oxen and four emigrant wagons rolled over the crest of the hill and gravely descended, while R—— rode in state in the van. It seems that during the process of shoeing the horse the smothered dissensions among the emigrants suddenly broke into open rupture. Some insisted on pushing forward, some on remaining where they were, and some on going back. Kearsley, their captain, threw up his command in disgust. "And now, boys," said he, "if any of you are for going ahead, just you come along with me."

Four wagons, with ten men, one woman, and one small child, made up the force of the "go-ahead" faction, and R——, with his usual proclivity [inclination] toward mischief, invited them to join our party. Fear of the Indians—for I can conceive no other motive—must have induced him to court so burdensome an alliance. At all events, the proceeding was a cool one. The men who joined us, it is true, were all that could be desired; rude [unrefined] indeed in manners, but frank, manly, and intelligent. To tell them we could not travel with them was out of the question. I merely reminded Kearsley that if his oxen could not keep up with our mules he must expect to be left behind, as we could not consent to be farther delayed on the journey; but he immediately replied that his oxen "*should* keep up; and if they couldn't, why, he allowed, he'd find out how to make 'em."

Compare Parkman's description of the emigrants with his description of the Indians. What different patterns of behavior does he find in each group? How does he seem to react to what he observes?

Pioneers making their way westward

Library of Congress

2
The Conquest

On the Oregon Trail

So far the land and the people, the mountains, deserts, and prairies, the Indians, trappers, and pioneers have been introduced. They are the cast of characters in the drama of the settling of the West. The next selections illustrate the ways in which the land was tamed and the wilderness brought under the hand of civilization. They describe the experience of crossing the country in a covered wagon and the terrible winter that the Donner Party spent in the Sierra Nevada Mountains. They also show through newspaper advertisements how people got to California by ship and tell the story of Chinese immigration to the United States. Finally there is an account of the Overland Stage by Mark Twain and a glimpse of the coming of the railroad, the event that spelled the end of the Old West.

Jesse Applegate Travels the Oregon Trail

The following account of life on the Oregon Trail was written by Jesse Applegate, who traveled West in 1843 with an emigrant train of sixty wagons and thousands of cattle. Perhaps five hundred persons journeyed with this caravan, which was well organized and well led, a bigger and better equipped expedition than the one Parkman met three years later (page 21). Here is a typical day on the trail:

It is four o'clock A.M.; the sentinels [guards] on duty have discharged their rifles—the signal that the hours of sleep are over; and every wagon and tent is pouring forth its night tenants, and slow-kindling smokes begin largely to rise and float away upon the morning air. Sixty men start from the corral, spreading as they make through the vast herd of cattle and horses that form a semi-circle around the encampment, the most distant perhaps two miles away.

The herders pass to the extreme verge [edge] and carefully examine for trails beyond, to see that none of the animals have strayed or been stolen during the night. This morning no trails lead beyond the outside animals in sight, and by five o'clock the herders begin to contract the great moving circle and the well-trained animals move slowly toward camp, clipping here and there a thistle or a tempting bunch of grass on the way. In about an hour five thousand animals are close up to the encampment, and the teamsters are busy selecting their teams and driving them inside the "corral" to be yoked. The corral is a circle one hundred yards deep, formed with wagons connected strongly with each other, the wagon in the rear being connected with the wagon in front by its tongue and ox chains. It is a strong barrier that the most vicious ox cannot break, and in case of an attack of the Sioux would be no contemptible entrenchment.

From six to seven o'clock is a busy time; breakfast is to be eaten, the tents struck, the wagons loaded, and the teams yoked and brought up in readiness to be attached to their respective wagons. All know when, at seven o'clock, the signal to march sounds, that those not ready to take their proper places in the line of march must fall into the dusty rear for the day.

At seven the bugle sounds and the group moves out, led by the pilot and his guards. Meantime, some members of the group form a hunting party to look for buffalo. It is from the viewpoint of the hunters on the bluffs of the river that the emigrant train is seen.

We are full six miles away from the line of march; though everything is dwarfed by distance, it is seen distinctly. The caravan has been about two hours in motion and is now as widely extended as a prudent regard for safety will permit. First, near the bank of the shining river, is a company of horsemen; they seem to have found an obstruction, for the main body has halted while three or four ride rapidly along the bank of the creek or slough. They are hunting a favorable crossing for the wagons; while we look they have succeeded; it has apparently required no work to make it passable, for all but one of the party have passed on and he has raised a flag, no doubt a signal to the wagons to steer their course to where he stands. The leading teamster sees him though he is yet two miles off, and steers his course directly towards him, all the wagons following in his track. They (the wagons) form a line three quarters of a mile in length; some of the teamsters ride upon the front of their wagons, some march beside their teams; scattered along the line companies of women and children are taking exercise on foot; they gather bouquets of rare and beautiful flowers that line the way; near them stalks a stately greyhound or an Irish wolf dog, apparently proud of keeping watch and ward over his master's wife and children.

Next comes a band of horses; two or three men or boys follow them, the docile and sagacious [wise] animals scarce needing this attention, for they have learned to follow in the rear of the wagons, and know that at noon they will be allowed to graze and rest. Their knowledge of time seems as accurate as of the place they are to occupy in the line, and even a full-blown thistle will scarcely tempt them to straggle or halt until the dinner hour has arrived. Not so with the large herd of horned beasts that bring up the rear; lazy, selfish and unsocial, it has been a task to get them in motion; the strong, always ready to domineer over the weak, halt in front and forbid the weaker to pass them. They seem to move only in fear of the driver's whip; though in the morning full to repletion [excess], they have not been driven an hour before their hunger and thirst seem to indicate a fast of days' duration. Through all the long day their greed is never satisfied, nor their thirst quenched, nor is there a moment of relaxation of the tedious and vexatious labors of their drivers, although to all others the march furnishes some season of relaxation or enjoyment. For the cow-drivers there is none. . . .

The pilot, by measuring the ground and timing the speed of the wagons and the walk of his horses, has determined the rate of each, so as to enable him to select the nooning place, as near as the requisite [necessary] grass and water can be had at the end of five hours' travel of the wagons. Today, the ground being favorable, little time has been lost in preparing the road, so that he and his pioneers are at the nooning place an hour in advance of the wagons, which time is spent in preparing convenient watering places for the animals and digging little wells near the bank of the Platte. As the teams are not unyoked, but simply turned loose from the wagons, a corral is not formed at noon, but the wagons are drawn up in columns, four abreast, the leading wagon of each platoon on the left—the platoons being formed with that view. This brings friends together at noon as well as at night. . . .

It is now one o'clock; the bugle has sounded, and the caravan has resumed its westward journey. It is in the same order, but the evening is far less animated than the morning march; a drowsiness has fallen apparently on man and beast; teamsters drop asleep on their perches and even when walking by their teams, and the words of command are now addressed to the slowly creeping oxen in the softened teror of women or the piping treble of children, while the snores of teamsters make a droning accompaniment.

As the sun goes down, the pilot halts the column for the night. The evening meal is prepared, guards take their places, and another day of the march comes to an end.

Why is the presence of so many animals a sign of good planning? What were the uses of the animals?

In the Sierras

The hardships of the trail took their toll from the west-bound settlers. A party of emigrants headed by George Donner started out for California from Illinois in the summer of 1846 and reached the Sierra Nevada Mountains in October after the winter snows had begun. Snowed in at what is now Donner Lake, twelve hundred feet below the pass, this group slowly starved to death. Only forty-eight of the original eighty-seven were left when rescue parties broke through to them in February. Some of them even turned to cannibalism to survive.

Virginia Reed Murphy Recalls the Donner Party's Ordeal

The following narrative, which does not mention cannibalism, describes that terrible winter. The author is Virginia Reed Murphy, who as a child lived through the ordeal.

Snow was already falling, although it was only the last week in October. Winter had set in a month earlier than usual. All trails and roads were covered, and our only guide was the summit, which it seemed we would never reach. Despair drove many nearly frantic. Each family tried to cross the mountains but found it impossible. When it was seen that the wagons could not be dragged through the snow, their goods and provisions were packed on oxen and another start was made, men and women walking in snow up to their waists, carrying their children in their arms and trying to drive their cattle. The Indians said they could find no road; so a halt was called, and Stanton went ahead with the guides and came back and reported that we could get across if we kept right on, but that it would be impossible if [more] snow fell. He was in favor of a forced march until the other side of the summit should be reached, but some of our party were so tired and exhausted with the day's labor that they declared they could not take another step; so the few who knew the danger that the night might bring yielded to the many, and we camped within three miles of the summit.

That night came the dreaded snow. Around the campfires under the trees great feathery flakes came whirling down. The air was so full of them that one could see objects only a few feet away. . . . With heavy hearts we turned back to a cabin that had been built . . . on the shore of a lake, since known as Donner Lake. The Donners were camped in Alder Creek Valley below the lake. . . . The snow came on so suddenly that they had no time to build cabins, but hastily put up brush sheds, covering them with pine boughs. . . .

Many attempts were made to cross the mountains, but all who tried were driven back by the pitiless storms. Finally a party was organized, since known as the "Forlorn Hope." They made snow-shoes, and fifteen started—ten men and five women—but only seven lived to reach California; eight men perished. They were over a month on the way, and the horrors endured by that Forlorn Hope no pen can describe nor imagination conceive. . . .

The misery endured during those four months at Donner Lake in our little dark cabins under the snow would fill pages and make the coldest heart ache. Christmas was near, but to the starving its memory gave no comfort. It came and passed without observance, but my mother had determined weeks before that her children should have a treat on this one day. She had laid away a few dried apples, some beans, a bit of tripe [meat], and a small piece of bacon. When this hoarded store was brought out, the delight of the little ones knew no bounds. The cooking was watched carefully, and when we sat down to our Christmas dinner, Mother said, "Children, eat slowly, for this one day you can have all you wish." . . .

The storms would often last ten days at a time, and we would have to cut chips from the logs inside which formed our cabins in order to start a fire. We could scarcely walk, and the men had hardly strength to procure wood. We would drag ourselves through the snow from one cabin to another, and some mornings snow would have to be shoveled out of the fireplace before a fire could be made. Poor little children were crying with hunger, and mothers were crying because they had so little to give to their children. We seldom thought of bread, we had been without it so long. . . .

Time dragged slowly along till we were no longer on short allowance but were simply starving. My mother determined to make an effort to cross the mountains. She could not see her children die without trying to get them food. It was hard to leave them, but she felt that it must be done. She told them she would bring them bread, so they were willing to stay, and with no guide but a compass we started—my mother, Eliza, Milt Elliot, and myself. Milt wore snow-shoes, and we followed in his tracks. We were five days in the mountains; Eliza gave out the first day and had to return, but we kept on and climbed one high mountain after another only to see others higher still ahead. Often I would have to crawl up the mountains, being too tired to walk . . . we were compelled to return, and just in time, for that night a storm came on, the most fearful of the winter, and we should have perished had we not been in the cabins.

We now had nothing to eat but raw hides, and they were on the roof of the cabin to keep out the snow; when prepared for cooking and boiled they were simply a pot of glue. When the hides were taken off our cabin and we were left without shelter, Mr. Breen gave us a home with his family, and Mrs. Breen prolonged my life by slipping me little bits of meat now and then when she discovered that I could not eat the hide. Death had already claimed many in our party, and it seemed as though relief never would reach us. Baylis Williams, who had been in delicate health before we left Springfield, was the first to die; he passed away before starvation had really set in. . . .

On his arrival at Sutter's Fort my father [the author's father had led another effort to cross the mountains to get help] made known the situation of the emigrants, and Captain [John] Sutter offered at once to do everything possible for their relief. He furnished horses and provisions, and my father and Mr. McClutchen started for the mountains, coming as far as possible with horses and then with packs on their backs proceeding on foot; but they were finally compelled to return. Captain Sutter was not surprised at their defeat. He stated that there were no able-bodied men in that vicinity, all having gone down the country with Frémont to fight the Mexicans. He advised my father to go to Yerba Buena, now San Francisco, and make his case known to the naval officer in command. My father was in fact conducting parties there—when the seven members of the Forlorn Hope arrived from across the mountains. Their famished faces told the story. Cattle were killed and men were up all night, drying beef and making flour by hand mills, nearly two hundred pounds being made in one night, and a party of seven, commanded by Captain Reasen P. Tucker, were sent to our relief by Captain Sutter and the alcalde [mayor], Mr. Sinclair. On the evening of February 19, 1847, they reached our cabins, where all were starving. They shouted to attract attention. Mr. Breen clambered up the icy steps from our cabin, and soon we heard the blessed words, "Relief, thank God, relief!"

Do you find it surprising that women were included in the Forlorn Hope group? Why or why not? What do this and preceding selections suggest to you about the role of women in the westward movement?

To California by Sea

The coast of California was first explored by the Spaniard Juan Cabrillo in 1542, but it was not until the time of the American Revolution that Spain established effective political control as far north as San Francisco. For the next three-quarters of a century most of California was first under Spain and then under Mexico. One month before the United States acquired California in 1848 following the war with Mexico, gold was discovered, and from then on California grew very rapidly. Eastern merchant ships long had traded with Spanish and Mexican California, carrying manufactured goods west and returning with hides. By 1848, when everyone wanted to go to California, oceangoing steamships were common. The quickest way, though expensive, to get to California was to take a steamer from New York to Panama, cross the isthmus by rail, then re-embark on another ship for San Francisco.

New York Shipping Lines Compete for Passengers

In the following advertisements from a New York City newspaper, all on the same day in 1852, shipping lines compete for business and describe how people can get to California quickly.

THROUGH TO SAN FRANCISCO—AT REDUCED RATES.—NEW YORK AND SAN FRANCISCO STEAMSHIP LINE.—The new steamship UNITED STATES, CHARLES C. BERRY, Commander, will take her departure for ASPINWALL, Navy-bay, on FRIDAY, July 2, at 3 P.M., connecting at Panama with the new double-engine steamship WINFIELD SCOTT, 2,100 tons burden, KENNEY COUILLARD, Commander, which steamer awaits the arrival of passengers at Panama by the UNITED STATES from New York, and immediately thereafter proceeds to San Francisco direct, without stopping at intermediate posts. These vessels, in accommodations and safety, are not surpassed by any on this route, and an experienced surgeon is attached to each vessel. The UNITED STATES has made the voyage between New York and

Chagres in 7 days and 19 hours, and the WINFIELD SCOTT performed the voyage between New York and Panama in the shortest time on record, both as to running and actual time from port to port. Books are now open, and through tickets for sale. Apply to

DAVIS, BROOKS & CO., General Agents,
No. 28 Beaver St., New York.
JONES & JOHNSTON, No. 104 West St.,
corner of Liberty St.

Passengers per UNITED STATES will disembark alongside the wharf at Aspinwall, and take the Panama Railroad, now opened nearly to Gorgona, thus avoiding the risk attendant upon landing in boats at Chagres, and the River navigation to Gorgona.

VANDERBILT'S LINE FOR SAN FRANCISCO.

THE SHORTEST AND CHEAPEST ROUTE—THE ONLY LINE GIVING TICKETS FOR CROSSING THE ISTHMUS—The favorite double engine Steamship PROMETHEUS, 1800 tons burden, will leave from Pier No. 2 North River, at 3 o'clock P.M. precisely, on SATURDAY, June 19, for San Juan del Norte, connecting with the Pacific steamer, over the Nicaragua Transit Route, having but 12 miles of land transportation. These steamers are unsurpassed in their Cabin or Steerage accommodations, and with the increased facilities for crossing, passengers may be assured of going through without detention at any point. This route offers superior advantages for Families going to California, as they are constantly under the charge of officers attached to the line. For information or passage apply only to

D. B. ALLEN, Agent, No. 9 Battery-place, up stairs.

San Francisco Bay in 1846

National Archives

Chinese Immigrants Arrive in San Francisco

Many of those who went to California by ship were fairly prosperous, but the Chinese immigrants who poured into San Francisco were poor people who came on a credit-ticket system and worked off the cost of their passage after arriving. The early arrivals came to look for gold, but they were badly treated by other miners who did not want competition, and gradually they settled in towns and cities and became traders and servants.

In the following selection a Hungarian immigrant, János Xánthus, writes a letter to his mother back in Hungary about life in San Francisco. He is particularly interested in the Chinese community.

San Francisco, California, May 5, 1857

Dear mother,

On the first of this month I wrote you a letter in which, aside from the detailed description of my journey, I let you know that I arrived here on the eve of April 30. Although I cannot give you much news, still I want to write you some lines, all the more because the post is leaving this evening on the ship *Golden Gate*, back to the States and Europe. . . .

The population of the town, 84,000 people, consists of a mixture from all nations of the world, but still it can be divided into four main classes in which the rest, an insignificant minority, is dissolved. One-fourth (in round figures) is of English tongue, one-fourth French and Spanish, one-fourth German, and one-fourth Chinese.

These last are in a peculiar position. In 1848, when gold was discovered in California, San Francisco had only 1200, and all California only 12,000 inhabitants; but miners needed working hands, because white workers were dear, and because slavery was prohibited. This directed the attention of the moneyed men to the great proletariat [masses] of China; they sent many ships there and imported within a few years 40,000 Chinamen, who worked very cheaply in the beginning, but later on, when they became acquainted with conditions here, they asked for higher and higher wages, and soon they worked only for as much salary as the white people.

So the sons of the Celestial Empire [China] have come gradually to affluence, and have fought themselves into an independent position. At present, in San Francisco alone, there are 22,000 in a separate quarter of the town, where they are to be seen in every possible type of shop. They have three newspapers issued in Chinese, an opera house, and a dance hall. The most remarkable thing is that they have kept their original costume and do not seem to show any disposition to adapt it to the local civilization.

If one walks in their quarter, one may easily think that he is in China; in front of all the shops, on the houses, and so on, there are Chinese ideograms [symbols] in the most glaring colors, and the Chinese language and music are heard every now and then. The sons and daughters of the Celestial Empire stroll up and down, wearing, without discrimination of sex, small pointed caps, wide coats, wide trousers, and thick-soled sandals, and having long pigtails reaching almost to the ground.

Although Xánthus sees the colorful aspects of Chinese culture, there were ugly sides of the Chinese immigration. When the Chinese were driven out of the mining camps, some were hired to build the Central Pacific Railroad, and thousands of others were imported as coolie labor to work on the railroad. They were exploited by the ship owners who overloaded their vessels and by the railroad builders.

A Government Agent Protests the Overloading of Immigrant Ships

The following letter was written on August 1, 1854, to the secretary of the treasury by J. Ross Browne, who was stationed in San Francisco.

Sir:

I desire to call your attention to the repeated violations of the Fassenger Acts of Feb. 22nd 1867 and May 17th 1848, which have recently taken place in the carrying of Chinese emigrants from the ports of China to San Francisco. The evil has now become so great as [to] create serious alarm on the part of the municipal and state authorities; and there is every prospect that it will be greatly augmented under the decisions of Judge Hoffman, by which the passenger laws are rendered a nullity. . . .

Vessels coming into port now carry from one to two passengers for every ton, and the result is that large numbers of them die on the passage and in port. The case of the *Libertad* can scarcely be surpassed in all its inhuman and disgusting details by that of any slaver in the African slave trade. . . .

It is now understood that . . . vessels are preparing to come over and some actually [are] on the way with upwards of a thousand passengers in each. An epidemic which will force the people of California to rise up in self-defense against these violations of law and humanity must be the consequence, unless active measures are taken to prevent further abuse of this kind. . . .

Very respectfully,
Your Ob[edien]t Serv[an]t,
J. Ross Browne

What were some of the differences between the Chinese and other immigrants? What comparisons can you make between the experiences of the Chinese and the blacks in this country?

With the Overland Stage

The career of Mark Twain as a river pilot ended when the Civil War stopped steamboat traffic on the Mississippi. He then joined his brother, who was going to Carson City, Nevada, to be secretary to the governor of the territory. The brothers took a steamboat up the Missouri River to Saint Joseph, where they caught the Overland Stage.

Mark Twain Travels by Stagecoach

Mark Twain's account of his trip to Nevada is a memorable picture of stagecoach travel across the prairies and mountains just eight years before the railroads made the Overland Stage obsolete. Here is a selection from *Roughing It:*

It was now just dawn; and as we stretched our cramped legs full length on the mail sacks, and gazed out through the windows across the wide wastes of greensward [grass] clad in cool, powdery mist, to where there was an expectant look in the eastern horizon, our perfect enjoyment took the form of a tranquil and contented ecstacy. The stage whirled along at a spanking gait, the breeze flapping curtains and suspended coats in a most exhilarating way; the cradle swayed and swung luxuriously, the pattering of the horses' hoofs, the cracking of the driver's whip, and his "Hi-yi! g'lang!" were music; the spinning ground and the waltzing trees appeared to give us a mute hurrah as we went by, and then slack up and look after us with interest, or envy, or something; and as we lay and smoked the pipe of peace and compared all this luxury with the years of tiresome city life that had gone before it, we felt that there was only one complete and satisfying happiness in the world, and we had found it.

After breakfast, at some station whose name I have forgotten, we three climbed up on the seat behind the driver, and let the conductor have our bed for a nap. And by and by, when the sun made me drowsy, I lay down on my face on top of the coach, grasping the slender iron railing, and slept for an hour more. That will give one an appreciable idea of those matchless roads. Instinct will make a sleeping man grip a fast hold of the railing when the stage jolts, but when it only swings and sways, no grip is necessary. Overland drivers and conductors used to sit in their places and sleep thirty or forty minutes at a time, on good roads, while spinning along at the rate of eight or ten miles an hour. I saw them do it, often. There was no danger about it; a sleeping man *will* seize the irons in time when the coach jolts. These men were hard worked, and it was not possible for them to stay awake all the time.

By and by we passed through Marysville, and over the Big Blue and Little Sandy; thence about a mile, and entered Nebraska. About a mile further on, we came to the Big Sandy—one hundred and eighty miles from St. Joseph.

When night comes, the passengers smooth out the mailbags inside the stagecoach and put on all their heavy clothes to protect themselves against the chilly weather. Then they go to sleep with their pistols and water canteens within reach. They have stowed a big dictionary amont the mailbags.

Whenever the stage stopped to change horses, we would wake up, and try to recollect where we were—and succeed—and in a minute or two the stage would be off again, and we likewise. We began to get into country, now, threaded here and there with little streams. These had high, steep banks on each side, and every time we flew down one bank and scrambled up the other, our party inside got mixed somewhat. First we would all be down in a pile at the forward end of the stage, nearly in a sitting posture, and in a second we would shoot to the other end, and stand on our heads. And we would sprawl and kick, too, and ward off ends and corners of mailbags that came lumbering over us and about us; and as the

Adventurous travelers on the Overland Stage

National Archives

dust rose from the tumult, we would all sneeze in chorus, and the majority of us would grumble, and probably say some hasty thing, like: "Take your elbow out of my ribs!—can't you quit crowding?"

Every time we avalanched from one end of the stage to the other, the Unabridged Dictionary would come too; and every time it came it damaged somebody. One trip it "barked" the Secretary's elbow; the next trip it hurt me in the stomach, and the third it tilted Bemis's nose up till he could look down his nostrils—he said. The pistols and coin soon settled to the bottom, but the pipes, pipe-stems, tobacco and canteens clattered and floundered after the Dictionary every time it made an assault on us, and aided and abetted the book by spilling tobacco in our eyes, and water down our backs.

Still, all things considered, it was a very comfortable night. It wore gradually away, and when at last a cold gray light was visible through the puckers and chinks in the curtains, we yawned and stretched with satisfaction, shed our cocoons, and felt that we had slept as much as was necessary. By and by, as the sun rose up and warmed the world, we pulled off our clothes and got ready for breakfast. We were just pleasantly in time, for five minutes afterward the driver sent the weird music of his bugle winding over the grassy solitudes, and presently we detected a low hut or two in the distance. Then the rattling of the coach, the clatter of our six horses' hoofs, and the driver's crisp commands, awoke to a louder and stronger emphasis, and we went sweeping down on the station at our smartest speed. *It was fascinating— that old Overland stagecoaching.*

What were the pleasures and discomforts of stagecoach travel? How do these compare with long-distance travel by train or bus today?

At Promontory Point, Utah

One of the dramatic events of American history took place at Promontory Point, Utah, on May 10, 1869. It was an event that brought the curtain down on the drama of the Old West. On that day a golden spike was driven into the last stretch of track, and for the first time the East and West were linked by a railroad. After the spike-driving ceremony, the engineer of the Central Pacific, which had started east from San Francisco, and the engineer of the Union Pacific, which had been built west from the Mississippi, ran their engines up until they touched. Then they shook hands and each broke a champagne bottle over the other's locomotive. There were speeches before and after, as gangs of Irish and Chinese laborers joined governors, railroad officials, and other notables in celebrating the great occasion.

Walt Whitman Writes of the Transcontinental Railroad

To Walt Whitman "tying the Eastern to the Western sea" had a highly emotional significance. It came in the same year that the Suez Canal was opened, and for Whitman the two events marked a great step forward in the advance of civilization. In his poem, "A Passage to India," Whitman writes of the transcontinental railroad:

I see over my own continent the Pacific railroad surmounting every barrier,
I see continual trains of cars winding along the Platte carrying freight and passengers,
I hear the locomotives rushing and roaring, and the shrill steam-whistle,
I hear the echoes reverberate through the grandest scenery in the world,
I cross the Laramie plains, I note the rocks in grotesque shapes, the buttes,
I see the plentiful larkspur and wild onions, the barren, colorless, sage-deserts,
I see in glimpses afar or towering immediately above me the great mountains, I see the Wind river and the Wahsatch mountains,
I see the Monument mountain and the Eagle's Nest, I pass the Promontory, I ascend the Nevadas,
I scan the noble Elk mountain and wind around its base,
I see the Humboldt range, I thread the valley and cross the river,
I see the clear waters of lake Tahoe, I see forests of majestic pines,
Or crossing the great desert, the alkaline plains, I behold enchanting mirages of waters and meadows,
Marking through these and after all, in duplicate slender lines,
Bridging the three or four thousand miles of land travel,
Tying the Eastern to the Western sea,
The road between Europe and Asia.

What emotional significance does the transcontinental railroad seem to have for Whitman? What does he mean in saying that it is "the road between Europe and Asia"?

Samuel Bowles Travels on the Union Pacific

During the summer before the transcontinental railroad was finished, the editor of the Springfield, Massachusetts, *Republican,* Samuel Bowles, visited the West. He traveled over the Union Pacific from Omaha, which he noted had become a boom town since he had visited it last in 1865. He describes his ride along the same route followed by the Oregon Trail and the Overland Stage.

Meeting of the Rails, 1869

U.S. DEPT. OF TRANSPORTATION/Federal Highway Admin.

The day's ride grows monotonous. The road is as straight as an arrow. Every dozen or fifteen miles is a station—two or three sheds, and a waterspout and wood-pile; every one hundred miles or so a home or a division depot, with shops, eating-house, "saloons" uncounted, a store or two, a few cultivated acres, and the invariable half-a-dozen seedy [untidy], staring loafers, that are a sort of fungi indigenous to American railways. We yawn over the unchanging landscape and the unvarying model of the stations, and lounge and read by day, and go to bed early at night. But the clear, dry air charms; the half dozen soldiers hurriedly marshalled into line at each station, as the train comes up, suggest that the Indian question is not disposed of yet; we catch a glimpse of antelopes in the distance; and we watch the holes of the prairie dogs for their piquant little owners and their traditional companions of owls and snakes—but never see the snakes.

The Plains proper and the first day's ride end at Cheyenne, five hundred and sixteen miles from Omaha. Here a branch road goes off south a hundred miles to Denver, where it connects with the St. Louis or Eastern Division of the Pacific road. Cheyenne is also a great railroad work and supply shop, as becomes its location adjoining the mountain and winter-exposed section of the road.

Bowles continues on across Wyoming to the end of the

line, which then is crossing the high, arid tablelands near Rawlins. He sees the track being laid over the Continental Divide at the top of the Rocky Mountains and marvels at the speed with which the job is being done. By the next May the construction crews have laid another 250 miles of track to complete the work.

Within this desert of the mountains, the divide of the continent occurs both on the old stage road and the new Railroad line; and here, in the summer of 1868, we witnessed the building of the track over the parting of the waters. The last rail on the Atlantic slope and the first on the Pacific were laid in our presence; and Governor Bross pinned them down with stalwart blows upon their spikes. As yet, still, no mountains appear in the path of the track, and it winds easily along through these rolling sand-hills, occasionally helped over a deep dry gulch, and spanning a feeble or possible river. But the whole section is mountainously high, from seven thousand to eight thousand feet above the sea level.

We witnessed here the fabulous speed with which the Railroad was built. Through the two or three hundred miles beyond were scattered ten to fifteen thousand men in great gangs preparing the road bed; plows, scrapers, shovels, picks and carts; and, among the rocks, drills and powder were doing the grading as rapidly as men could stand and move with their tools. Long trains brought up to the end of the completed track loads of ties and rails; the former were transferred to teams, sent one or two miles ahead, and put in place upon the grade. Then rails and spikes were reloaded on platform cars, these pushed up to the last previously laid rail, and with an automatic movement and a celerity [speed] that were wonderful, practiced hands dropped the fresh rails one after another on the ties exactly in line, huge sledges sent the spikes home, the car rolled on, and the operation was repeated; while every few minutes the long heavy train behind sent out a puff from its locomotive, and caught up with its load of material the advancing work. The only limit, inside of eight miles in twenty-four hours, to the rapidity with which the track could thus be laid, was the power of the road behind to bring forward the materials.

As the Railroad marched thus rapidly across the broad Continent of plain and mountain, there was improvised a rough and temporary town at its every public stopping-place. As this was changed every thirty or forty days, these settlements were of the most perishable materials—canvas tents, plain board shanties, and turf-hovels [sod huts]—pulled down and sent forward for a new career, or deserted as worthless, at every grand movement of the Railroad company. Only a small proportion of their populations had aught to do with the road, or any legitimate occupation. Most were the hangers-on around the disbursements of such a gigantic work, catching the drippings from the feast in any and every form that it was possible to reach them. Restaurant and saloon keepers, gamblers, desperadoes [criminals] of every grade, the vilest of men and of women made up this "Hell on Wheels," as it was most aptly termed.

Who helped build the railroads? Where do you think the people came from? Where were they going? In your opinion who benefited most by the building of the transcontinental railroad? Why?

Off and On the Reservation

The conquest of the West was also the conquest of the Indians, either by killing them or by confining them to reservations. Where Indians and settlers clashed, United States military forces, generally cavalry units, moved in to subdue the Indians. There was treachery on both sides, and frequent disagreement about the meaning of treaties.

Geronimo, an Apache, was one of the last Indian war leaders to be overcome. In 1876 when the federal government forced the Apaches onto an Arizona reservation, he escaped with a small band of followers and hid in the mountains of Mexico. The band terrorized ranchers on both sides of the border and fought a guerrilla war against thousands of United States and Mexican troops for ten years, until forced to surrender by Gen. Nelson A. Miles. Geronimo ended his days as a prisoner of war, and prosperous farmer, at Fort Sill in Oklahoma.

Geronimo Tells His Story of Rebellion and Submission

The following selection is from *Geronimo's Story of His Life,* which the Apache dictated to S.M. Barrett.

We were reckless of our lives, because we felt that every man's hand was against us. If we returned to the reservation we would be put in prison and killed; if we stayed in Mexico they would continue to send soldiers to fight us; so we gave no quarter to anyone and asked no favors. . . .

Contrary to our expectations the United States soldiers had not left the mountains in Mexico, and were soon trailing us and skirmishing with us almost every day. Four or five times they surprised our camp. One time they surprised us about nine o'clock in the morning, and captured all our horses (nineteen in number) and secured our store of dried meats. We also lost three Indians in this encounter. About the middle of the afternoon of the same day we attacked them from the rear as they were passing through a prairie—killed one soldier, but lost none ourselves. In this skirmish we recovered all our horses except three that belonged to me. The three horses that we did not recover were the best riding horses we had.

Soon after this we made a treaty with the Mexican troops. They told us that the United States troops were the real cause of these wars, and agreed not to fight any more with us provided we would return to the United States. This we agreed to do, and resumed our march, expecting to try to make a treaty with the United States soldiers and return to Arizona. There seemed to be no other course to pursue. . . .

When we had made the treaty General Miles said to me: "My brother, you have in your mind how you are going to kill men, and other thoughts of war; I want you to put that out of your mind, and change your thoughts to peace."

Then I agreed and gave up my arms. I said: "I will quit the warpath and live at peace hereafter."

Then General Miles swept a spot of ground clear with his hand, and said: "Your past deeds shall be wiped out like this and you will start a new life."

When I had given up to the Government they put me on the Southern Pacific Railroad and took me to San Antonio, Texas, and held me to be tried by their laws.

In forty days they took me from there to Fort Pickens (Pensacola), Florida. Here they put me to sawing up large logs. There were several other Apache warriors with me, and all of us had to work every day. For nearly two years we were kept at hard labor in this place and we did not see our families until May, 1887. This treatment was in direct violation of our treaty made at Skeleton Cañon.

After this we were sent with our families to Vermont, Alabama, where we stayed five years and worked for the Government. We had no property, and I looked in vain for General Miles to send me to that land of which he had spoken; I longed in vain for the implements, house, and stock that General Miles had promised me. . . .

When we first came to Fort Sill [a military reservation where Indians were being trained in agriculture], Captain Scott was in charge, and he had houses built for us by the Government. We were also given, from the Government, cattle, hogs, turkeys and chickens. The Indians did not do much good with the hogs, because they did not understand how to care for them, and not many Indians even at the present time keep hogs. We did better with the turkeys and chickens, but with these we did not have as good luck as white men do. With the cattle we have done very well, indeed, and we like to raise them. We have a few horses also, and have had no bad luck with them.

How can you explain the treatment of the band as prisoners of war? At this late date in the advance of western settlement, what choices were available to the Indians? What is your opinion of Geronimo's rebellion? Why?

Saturday in a western town — Library of Congress

3
The Mining Frontier

The Discovery of Gold

Gold was discovered in January, 1848, on a ranch owned by John Sutter on the American River in northern California. He was the same Sutter whose ranch was sought out by Frémont and the Donner party. News of the find spread like a prairie fire, and California, which had been a sparsely populated land of cattle ranchers, became the Mecca of gold-seekers. Everyone who was lucky enough to be on the Pacific Coast rushed to the foothills of the Sierras to hunt for gold, and as soon as the news reached the East Coast, thousands of emigrants by land and by sea joined the gold rush.

In the years that followed the California gold rush, other rich deposits of precious metals were found elsewhere in the West. The Comstock Lode in Nevada produced a fabulous amount of silver, and later strikes in Colorado made boom towns out of Denver, Cripple

Creek, and Central City. Still another gold rush after the Civil War took place in the Black Hills of South Dakota.

The following selections give three glimpses of the rush for precious metals. The first two recount gold rush days in California; the third deals with the silver bonanza in Nevada.

Walter Colton Describes the Effect of the Discovery

The Reverend Walter Colton, a Congregational minister, arrived in California in 1846 just after the Americans had taken possession of Monterey. He was preaching and serving as alcalde of Monterey at the time gold was discovered. The following paragraphs come from his book, *Three Years in California*.

Monday, May 29, 1848: Our town was startled out of its quiet dreams today by the announcement that gold had been discovered on the American Fork. The men wondered and talked, and the women too; but neither believed. . . .

Monday, June 12: A straggler came in today from the American Fork bringing a piece of yellow ore weighing an ounce. . . . But doubts still hovered on the minds of the great mass. They could not conceive that such a treasure could have lain there so long undiscovered. . . .

Tuesday, June 20: My messenger sent to the mines has returned with specimens of the gold; he dismounted in a sea of upturned faces. As he drew forth the yellow lumps from his pockets, and passed them around among the eager crowd, the doubts, which had lingered till now, fled. All admitted they were gold, except one old man, who still persisted they were some Yankee invention, got up to reconcile [win the acceptance of] the people to the change of flag. The excitement produced was intense; and many were soon busy in their hasty preparations for a departure to the mines. The family who had kept house for me caught the moving infection. Husband and wife were both packing up; the blacksmith dropped his hammer, the carpenter his plane, the mason his trowel, the farmer his sickle, the baker his loaf, and the tapster [bartender] his bottle. All were off for the mines, some on horses, some on carts, and some on crutches, and one went in a litter [stretcher]. An American woman, who had recently established a boarding-house here, pulled up stakes, and was off before her lodgers had even time to pay their bills. Debtors ran, of course. I have only a community of women left, and a gang of prisoners, with here and there a soldier, who will give his captain the slip at the first chance. I don't blame the fellow a whit; seven dollars a month, while others are making two or three hundred a day! that is too much for human nature to stand.

Saturday, July 15: The gold fever has reached every servant in Monterey; none are to be trusted in their engagement beyond a week, and as for compulsion, it is like attempting to drive fish into a net with the ocean before them. Gen. Mason, Lieut. Lanman, and myself form a mess [eat together]; we have a house, and all the table furniture and culinary apparatus requisite; but our servants have run, one after another, till we are almost in despair . . . and this morning, for the fortieth time, we had to take to the kitchen and cook our own breakfast. A general of the United States Army, the commander of a man-of-war, and the Alcalde of Monterey in a smoking kitchen, grinding coffee, toasting a herring, and peeling onions!

What motives other than greed might make people join a gold rush? What do you think you would have done in 1848 and 1849? Why? Why does California today still attract great numbers of people? What, if any, similarity do you find between this population movement and the 1849 gold rush?

Bayard Taylor Visits the Mining Camps

When the news of the gold strike reached New York, Horace Greeley, editor of the *Tribune,* sent a reporter, Bayard Taylor, to visit the mining camps. Taylor, who later became a well-known poet and travel writer, reached San Francisco by sea in August, 1849. On his way to the diggings he passed through Stockton.

Our first visit to Stockton was made in company, on some of Major Graham's choicest horses. A mettled roan *canalo* fell to my share, and the gallop of five miles without check was most inspiring. A view of Stockton was something to be remembered. There, in the heart of California, where the last winter stood a solitary ranch in the midst of tule marches, I found a canvas town of a thousand inhabitants, and a port with twenty-five vessels at anchor! The mingled noises of labor around—the click of hammers and the grating of saws—the shouts of mule-drivers—the jingling of spurs—the jar and jostle of wares in the tents—almost cheated me into the belief that it was some old commercial mart, familiar with such sounds for years past. Four months, only, had sufficed to make the place what it was; and in that time a wholesale firm established there (one out of a dozen) had done business to the amount of $100,000. The same party had just purchased a lot of eighty by one hundred feet, on the principal street, for $6,000, and the cost of erecting a common one-story clapboard house on it was $15,000.

Taylor continues by mule from Stockton to the diggings on the Mokelumne River, some forty miles away. He is lodged in an open-air hotel which consists of two log tables, one for eating, the other for gambling. The morning after arriving he inspects the mining operations.

I slept soundly that night on the dining-table, and went down early to the river, where I found the party of ten bailing out the water which had leaked into the riverbed during the night. They were standing in the sun, and had two hours' hard work before they could begin to wash. Again the prospect looked uninviting, but when I went there again towards noon, one of them was scraping up the sand from the bed with his knife, and throwing it into a basin, the bottom of which glittered with gold. Every knifeful brought out a quantity of grains and scales, some of which were as large as the fingernail. At last a two-ounce lump fell plump into the pan, and the diggers, now in the best possible humor, went on with their work with great alacrity [eagerness]. Their forenoon's digging amounted to nearly six pounds [an ounce of gold in California was then worth $16.00]. It is only by such operations as these, through associated labor, that great profits are to be made in those districts which have been visited by the first eager horde of gold-hunters. The deposits most easily reached are soon exhausted by the crowd, and the labor required to carry on further work successfully deters single individuals from attempting it. Those who, retaining their health, return home disappointed say they have been humbugged [fooled] about the gold, when in fact they have humbugged themselves about the *work*. If anyone expects to dig treasures out of the earth, in California, without severe labor, he is woefully mistaken. Of all classes of men, those who pave streets and quarry limestone are best adapted for gold-diggers.

One of the principal mining operators at the Mokelumne River site, Dr. Gillette, tells Taylor how he and a companion struck it rich in a particular gulch nearby.

One day at noon, while resting in the shade of a tree, Dr. G. took a pick and began carelessly turning up the ground. Almost on the surface, he struck and threw out a lump of gold of about two pounds' weight. Inspired by this unexpected result, they both went to work, laboring all that day and the next, and even using part of the night to quarry out the heavy pieces of rock. At the end of the second day they went to the village on the Upper Bar and weighed their profits, which amounted to fourteen pounds! They started again the third morning under pretense of hunting, but were suspected and followed by the other diggers, who came upon them just as they commenced work. The news rapidly spread, and there was soon a large number of men on the spot, some of whom obtained several pounds per day, at the start. The gulch had been well dug up for the large lumps, but there was still great wealth in the earth and sand, and several operators only waited for the wet season to work it in a systematic manner.

The next day Colonel Lyons, Dr. Gillette, and myself set out on a visit to the scene of these rich discoveries. Climbing up the rocky bottom of the gulch, as by a staircase, for four miles, we found nearly every part of it dug up and turned over by the picks of the miners. Deep holes, sunk between the solid strata or into the precipitous sides of the mountains, showed where veins of the metal had been struck and followed as long as they yielded lumps large enough to pay for the labor. The loose earth, which they had excavated, was full of fine gold, and only needed washing out. A number of Sonorians [Mexicans] were engaged in dry-washing this refuse sand—work which requires no little skill, and would soon kill any other men than these lank and skinny Arabs of the West. Their mode of work is as follows: Gathering the loose dry sand in bowls, they raise it to their heads and slowly pour it upon a blanket spread at their feet. Repeating this several times, and throwing out the worthless pieces of rock, they reduce the dust to about half its bulk; then, balancing the bowl on one hand, by a quick, dexterous motion of the other they cause it to revolve, at the same time throwing its contents into the air and catching them as they fall. In this manner everything is finally winnowed [blown] away except the heavier grains of sand mixed with gold, which is carefully separated by the breath. It is a laborious occupation, and one which, fortunately, the American diggers have not attempted. This breathing the fine dust from day to day, under a more than torrid sun, would soon impair the strongest lungs.

We found many persons at work in the higher part of the gulch, searching for veins and pockets of gold, in the holes which had already produced their first harvest. Some of these gleaners [gatherers], following the lodes abandoned by others as exhausted, into the sides of the mountain, were well repaid for their perseverance. Others, again, had been working for days without finding anything. Those who understood the business obtained from one to four ounces daily. Their only tools were the crowbar, pick, and knife, and many of them, following the veins under strata of rock which lay deep below the surface, were obliged to work while lying flat on their backs, in cramped and narrow holes.

How do you account for the high cost of land and a house in Stockton? Why do you think that Taylor emphasizes the hard work and skill involved in digging for gold?

Mark Twain Doesn't Strike It Rich

As Bayard Taylor suggests in the preceding narrative, not all fortune-seekers in the mining camps succeeded in finding gold or silver. Many were unlucky or unwilling to work hard and returned home disillusioned. Most stayed in California, however, and became farmers or city workers. Thus California was settled before many states farther east. Mark Twain, who tried his hand at prospecting, was not a very serious miner and found his gold when he turned his western experiences into literary material, such as *Roughing It,* from which the next selection comes. Here he tells how he almost got rich.

I confess, without shame, that I expected to find masses of silver lying all about the ground. I expected to see it glittering in the sun on the mountain summits. I said nothing about this, for some instinct told me that I might possibly have an exaggerated idea about it, and so if I betrayed my thought I might bring derision [ridicule] upon myself. Yet I was as perfectly satisfied in my own mind as I could be of anything that I was going to gather up, in a day or two, or at furthest a week or two, silver enough to make me satisfactorily wealthy—and so my fancy was already busy with plans for spending this money. The first opportunity that offered, I sauntered carelessly away from the cabin, keeping an eye on the other boys, and stopping and contemplating the sky when they seemed to be observing me; but as soon as the coast was manifestly clear, I fled away as guiltily as a thief might have done and never halted till I was far beyond sight and call.

Then I began my search with a feverish excitement that was brimful of expectation—almost of certainty. I crawled about the ground, seizing and examining bits of stone, blowing the dust from them or rubbing them on my clothes, and then peering at them with anxious hope. Presently I found a bright fragment and my heart bounded! I hid behind a boulder and polished it and scrutinized it with a nervous eagerness and a delight that was more pronounced than absolute certainty itself could have afforded. The more I examined the fragment the more I was convinced that I had found the door to fortune. I marked the spot and carried away my specimen. Up and down the rugged mountain side I searched, with always increasing interest and always augmenting gratitude that I had come to Humboldt and come in time. Of all the experiences of my life, this secret search among the hidden treasures of silver-land was the nearest to unmarred ecstasy. It was a delirious revel [spree].

By and by, in the bed of a shallow rivulet, I found a deposit of shining yellow scales, and my breath almost forsook me! A gold mine, and in my simplicity I had been content with vulgar silver! I was so excited that I half believed my overwrought imagination was deceiving me. Then a fear came upon me that people might be observing me and would guess my secret. Moved by this thought, I made a circuit of the place, and ascended a knoll to reconnoiter [look around]. Solitude. No creature was near. Then I returned to my mine, fortifying myself against possible disappointment, but my fears were groundless—the shining scales were still there. I set about scooping them out, and for an hour I toiled down the windings of the stream and robbed its bed. But at last the descending sun warned me to give up the quest, and I turned homeward laden with wealth. As I walked along I could not help smiling at the thought of my being so excited over my fragment of silver when a nobler metal was almost under my nose. In this little time the former had so fallen in my estimation that once or twice I was on the point of throwing it away.

The boys were as hungry as usual, but I could eat nothing. Neither could I talk. I was full of dreams and far away. Their conversation interrupted the flow of my fancy somewhat, and annoyed me a little, too. I despised the sordid and commonplace things they talked about. But as they proceeded, it began to amuse me. It grew to be rare fun to hear them planning their poor little economies and sighing over possible privations and distresses [trials and troubles] when a gold mine, all our own, lay within sight of the cabin and I could point it out at any moment. Smothered hilarity began to oppress me, presently. It was hard to resist the impulse to burst out with exultation and reveal everything; but I did resist. I said within myself that I would filter the great news through my lips calmly and be serene as a summer morning while I watched its effect in their faces. I said:

"Where have you all been?"

"Prospecting."

"What did you find?"

"Nothing."

"Nothing? What do you think of the country?"

"Can't tell, yet," said Mr. Ballou, who was an old gold miner, and had likewise had considerable experience among the silver mines.

"Well, haven't you formed any sort of opinion?"

"Yes, a sort of one. It's fair enough here, maybe, but over-rated. Seven-thousand-dollar ledges are scarce, though. That Sheba may be rich enough, but we don't own it; and besides, the rock is so full of base metals that all the science in the world can't work it. We'll not starve, here, but we'll not get rich, I'm afraid."

"So you think the prospect is pretty poor?"

"No name for it!"

"Well, we'd better go back, hadn't we?"

"Oh, not yet—of course not. We'll try it a riffle, first."

"Suppose, now—this is merely a supposition, you know—suppose you could find a ledge that would yield, say, a hundred and fifty dollars a ton—would that satisfy you?"

"Try us once!" from the whole party.

"Or suppose—merely a supposition, of course—suppose you were to find a ledge that would yield two thousand dollars a ton—would *that* satisfy you?"

"Here—what do you mean? What are you coming at? Is there some mystery behind all this?"

"Never mind. I am not saying anything. You know perfectly well there are no rich mines here—of course you do. Because you have been around and examined for yourselves. Anybody would know that, that had been around. But just for the sake of argument, suppose—in a kind of general way—suppose some person were to tell you that two-thousand-dollar ledges were simply contemptible—contemptible, understand—and that right yonder in sight of this very cabin there were piles of pure gold and pure silver—oceans of it—enough to make you all rich in twenty-four hours! Come!"

"I should say he was as crazy as a loon!" said old Ballou, but wild with excitement, nevertheless.

"Gentlemen," said I, "I don't say anything—*I* haven't been around, you know, and of course don't know anything—but all I ask of you is to cast your eye on *that,* for instance, and tell me what you think of it!" and I tossed my treasure before them.

There was an eager scramble for it, and a closing of heads together over it under the candle-light. Then old Ballou said:

"Think of it? I think it is nothing but a lot of granite rubbish and nasty glittering mica that isn't worth ten cents an acre!"

So vanished my dream. So melted my wealth away. So toppled my airy castle to the earth and left me stricken and forlorn.

Moralizing, I observed, then, that "all that glitters is not gold."

Mr. Ballou said that I could go further than that, and lay it up among my treasures of knowledge, that *nothing* that glitters is gold. So I learned then, once for all, that gold in its native state is but dull, unornamental stuff, and that only lowborn metals excite the admiration of the ignorant with an ostentatious [flashy] glitter. However, like the rest of the world, I still go on underrating men of gold and glorifying men of mica. Commonplace human nature cannot rise above that.

What gave Mark Twain and other prospectors the notion that riches lay waiting for them? What is the twist that he gives to the end of the story?

Rest time during a cattle drive — Library of Congress

4 The Ranching Frontier

The Long Drive

Before the Texans won independence from Mexico, stocks of Spanish cattle owned by Mexicans ranged the plains of Southern Texas. Then the Mexicans were driven out, and their cattle ran wild. By the time of the Civil War, herds of wild longhorns roamed the Texas ranges. As the population of the United States grew and the railroads pushed across the West, the cattle industry became big business. Texas ranchers began rounding up the wild cattle and driving them to market over various trails, the best known of which probably is the Chisholm Trail from the Mexican border to the railroad at Abilene, Kansas. Ranching soon spread to other western states clear to the Canadian border. The three decades following the Civil War were the golden age of the cowboy.

Andy Adams Meets Rustlers

Andy Adams, who was born in Georgia of Scotch-Irish parents, moved to Texas after the Civil War. He grew up in the cattle country and naturally drifted into cow-punching as a career. When he was in his early twenties, he joined a long cattle drive from Texas to Montana under the leadership of a foreman named Jim Flood. The expedition, which he describes vividly in *The Log of a Cowboy*, began along the Rio Grande River in Texas in April, 1882. Six riders guarded either side of a long cow column that stretched out over three-quarters of a mile of crooked trail. The main problem until the herd reached the Colorado River in central Texas was to find watering places, but as the animals approached the river, the cowhands learned that rustlers were active in that area. Their chief worry was that the rustlers would sneak into their midst at night, stampede the cattle, and then drive off part of the herd under cover of darkness.

We camped that night some five or six miles back from the river on the last divide. From the time the second guard went on until the third was relieved, we took the precaution of keeping a scout outriding from a half to three quarters of a mile distant from the herd, Flood and Honeyman serving in that capacity. Every precaution was taken to prevent a surprise; and in case anything did happen, our night horses tied to the wagon wheels stood ready and saddled and bridled for any emergency. But the night passed without incident.

An hour or two after the herd had started the next morning, four well-mounted, strange men rode up from the westward, and representing themselves as trail cutters, asked for our foreman. Flood met them, in his usual quiet manner, and after admitting that we had been troubled more or less with range cattle, assured our callers that if there was anything in the herd in the brands they represented, he would gladly hold it up and give them every opportunity to cut their cattle out. As he was anxious to cross the river before noon, he invited the visitors to stay for dinner, assuring them that before starting the herd in the afternoon, he would throw the cattle together for their inspection. Flood made himself very agreeable, inquiring into cattle and range matters in general as well as the stage of water in the river ahead. The spokesman of the trail cutters met Flood's invitation to dinner with excuses about the pressing demands on his time, and urged, if it did not seriously interfere with our plans, that he be allowed to inspect the herd before crossing the river. His reasons seemed trivial and our foreman was not convinced.

"You see, gentlemen," he said, "in handling these southern cattle, we must take advantage of occasions. We have timed our morning's drive so as to reach the river during the warmest hour of the day, or as near noon as possible. You can hardly imagine what a difference there is, in fording this herd, between a cool, cloudy day and a clear, hot one. You see the herd is strung out nearly a mile in length now, and to hold them up and waste an hour or more for your inspection would seriously disturb our plans. And then our wagon and *remuda* [spare horses] have gone on with orders to noon at the first good camp beyond the river. I perfectly understand your reasons, and you equally understand mine; but I will send a man or two back to help you recross any cattle you may find in our herd. Now, if a couple of you gentlemen will ride around on the far side with me, and the others will ride up near the lead, we will trail the cattle across when we reach the river without cutting the herd into blocks."

Flood's affability [pleasantness], coupled with the fact that the lead cattle were nearly up to the river, won his point. Our visitors could only yield, and rode forward with our lead swing men to assist in forcing the lead cattle into the river. It was swift water, but otherwise an easy crossing, and we allowed the herd, after coming out on the farther side, to spread out and graze forward at its pleasure. The wagon and saddle stock were in sight about a mile ahead, and leaving two men on herd to drift the cattle in the right direction, the rest of us rode leisurely on to the wagon, where dinner was waiting. Flood treated our callers with marked courtesy during dinner, and casually inquired if any of their number had seen any cattle that day or the day previous in the Ellison road brand. They had not, they said, explaining that their range lay on both sides of the Concho, and that during the trail season they kept all their cattle between that river and the main Colorado. Their work had kept them on their own range recently, except when trail herds were passing and needed to be looked through for strays. It sounded as though our trail cutters could also use diplomacy on occasion.

When dinner was over and we had caught horses for the afternoon and were ready to mount, Flood asked our guests for their credentials [papers] as duly authorized trail cutters. They replied that they had none, but offered in explanation the statement that they were merely cutting in the interest of the immediate locality, which required no written authority.

Then the previous affability of our foreman turned into iron. "Well, men," said he, "if you have no authority to cut this trail, then you don't cut this herd. I must have inspection papers before I can move a brand out of the county in which it is bred, and I'll certainly let no other man, local or duly appointed, cut an animal out of this herd without written and certified authority. You know that without being told, or ought to. I respect the rights of every man posted on a trail to cut it. If you want to see my inspection papers, you have a right to demand them, and in turn I demand of you your credentials, showing who you work for and the list of brands you represent; otherwise no harm's done; nor do you cut any herd that I'm driving."

"Well," said one of the men, "I saw a couple of head in my own individual brand as we rode up the herd. I'd like to see the man who says that I haven't the right to claim my own brand, anywhere I find it."

"If there's anything in our herd in your individual brand," said Flood, "all you have to do is to give me the brand, and I'll cut it for you. What's your brand?"

"The 'Window Sash.' "

"Have any of you boys seen such a brand in our herd?" inquired Flood, turning to us as we all stood by our horses ready to start.

The strangers, who actually were rustlers, had hoped to bluff Flood out of some cattle. All herds traveling across unfenced range managed to pick up strays from time to time. When Flood would not let the strangers get away with their trick, they fell back on claiming cows with the "Window Sash" brand. Three such animals had found their way into the big herd as it moved north. After the rustlers angrily drove off their trio of scrawny cows, Flood met some Texas Rangers under the command of Corporal Hames. They laid a trap for the rustlers, who had threatened to return. When the rustlers did reappear with twenty other riders, Flood went out to meet them and at the same time sent a signal to the Rangers.

"Well, I'm as good as my word," said the leader, "and I'm here to trim your herd as I promised you I would. Throw off and hold up your cattle, or I'll do it for you."

Several of our outfit rode up at this juncture in time to hear Flood's reply: "If you think you're equal to the occasion, hold them up yourself. If I had as big an outfit as you have, I wouldn't ask any man to help me. I want to watch a Colorado River outfit work a herd—I might learn something. My outfit will take a rest, or perhaps hold the cut or otherwise clerk for you. But be careful and don't claim anything that you are not certain is your own, for I reserve the right to look over your cut before you drive it away."

The rustlers rode in a body to the lead, and when they had thrown the herd off the trail, about half of them rode back and drifted towards the rear cattle. Flood called our outfit to one side and gave us our instructions, the herd being entirely turned over to the rustlers. After they began cutting, we rode around and pretended to assist in holding the cut as the strays in our herd were being cut out. . . . Not a man of us even cast a glance up the trail, or in the direction of the Rangers; but when the work was over, Flood protested with the leader of the rustlers over some five or six head of dim-branded cattle which actually belonged to our herd. But he was exultant [overjoyed] and would listen to no protests, and attempted to drive away the cut, now numbering nearly fifty head. Then we rode across their front and stopped them. In the parley [discussion] which ensued, harsh words were passing, when one of our outfit blurted out in well-feigned surprise—

"Hello, who's that, coming over there?"

A squad of men were riding leisurely through our abandoned herd, coming over to where the two outfits were disputing.

"What's the trouble here, gents?" inquired Hames as he rode up.

"Who are you and what might be your business, may I ask?" inquired the leader of the rustlers.

"Personally I'm nobody, but officially I'm Corporal in Company B, Texas Rangers—well, if there isn't smiling Ed Winters, the biggest cattle thief ever born in Medina County. Why, I've got papers for you; for altering the brands on over fifty head of 'C' cattle into a 'G' brand. Come here, dear, and give me that gun of yours. Come on, and no false moves or funny work or I'll shoot the white out of your eye. Surround this layout, lads, and let's examine them more closely."

At this command, every man in our outfit whipped out his six-shooter, the Rangers leveled their carbines [rifles] on the rustlers, and in less than a minute's time they were disarmed and as crestfallen a group of men as ever walked into a trap of their own setting. Hames got out a "black book," and after looking the crowd over concluded to hold the entire covey, as the descriptions of the "wanted" seemed to include most of them. Some of the rustlers attempted to explain their presence, but Hames decided to hold the entire party, "just to learn them to be more careful of their company the next time," as he put it.

What qualities of leadership does Flood show? How does cooperation among the cowhands help in foiling the rustlers?

Solomor D. Butcher Collection/Nebraska State Historical Society

Homesteaders in front of their sod house

5
The Farming Frontier

Homesteading in the Dakotas

The last frontier to fall before the westward march of the settlers was that of the farmer. Farmers were beginning to plow the prairie soil even before the Civil War, but after that conflict the line of farming communities in Nebraska, Kansas, and the Dakotas began to move steadily westward. The railroads were given large tracts of public land which they sold to settlers. Many Civil War veterans took up free land after their discharge, as provided for in the Homestead Act of 1862. The following selections illustrate the farming frontier on the plains.

O.E. Rölvaag Pictures the Norwegian Settlers

O.E. Rölvaag, the author of the following selection, grew up in a Norwegian fishing village, but at the age of twenty he emigrated to America and worked for his uncle on a Dakota farm. Later he worked his way through Saint Olaf College and eventually became a professor of Norwegian literature. His excellent novel, *Giants in the Earth,* from which the following pages are taken, describes the life of Norwegian farmers in the Dakota Territory. As the novel opens, several Norwegian families are taking up homesteads. Before they make their first crops and can afford real houses, they have to live in sod houses, which are built of grass-covered earth.

On the side of a hill, which sloped gently away toward the southeast and followed with many windings a creek that wormed its way across the prairie, stood Hans Olsa, laying turf. He was building a sod house. The walls had now risen breast-high; in its half-finished condition, the structure resembled more a bulwark against some enemy than anything intended to be a human habitation. And the great heaps of cut sod, piled up in each corner, might well have been the stores of ammunition for defense of the stronghold. . . .

Beyond the house a tent had been pitched; a wagon was drawn up close beside it. On the ground outside of the tent stood a stove, a couple of chairs, and a few other rough articles of furniture. A stout, healthy-looking woman, whose face radiated an air of simple wisdom and kindliness, was busy preparing the midday meal. She sang to herself as she worked. A ten-year-old girl, addressed by the woman as Sofie, was helping her. Now and then the girl would take up the tune and join in the singing.

Less than a quarter of a mile away, in a southeasterly direction, a finished sod house rose on the slope of the hill. Smoke was winding up from it at this moment. This house, which had been built the previous fall, belonged to Syvert Tönseten.

Some distance north from the place where Hans Olsa had located, two other sod houses were under construction; but a hillock lay between, so that he could not see them from where he stood. There the two Solum boys had driven down their stakes and had begun building. Tönseten's completed house, and the other three half-finished ones, marked the beginning of the settlement on Spring Creek.

The woman who had been bustling about preparing the meal, now called to her husband that dinner was ready—he must come at once! He answered her, straightened up for the hundredth time, wiped his hands on his trousers, and stood for a moment gazing off eastward. . . . No use to look—not a soul in sight yet! . . . He sighed heavily, and walked with slow steps toward the tent, his eyes on the ground.

It was light and airy inside the tent, but stifling hot, because of the unobstructed sunlight beating down upon it. Two beds were ranged along the wall, both of them homemade; a big emigrant chest stood at the head of each. Nails had been driven into the center pole of the tent, on which hung clothing; higher up a crosspiece, securely fastened, was likewise hung with clothes. Two of the walls were lined with furniture; on these pieces the dishes were displayed, all neatly arranged.

A large basin of water stood on a chair just inside the tent door. Hans Olsa washed his face and hands; then he came out and sat down on the ground, where his wife had spread the table. It was so much cooler outside. The meal was all ready; both mother and daughter had been waiting for him.

"I suppose you haven't seen any signs of them yet?" his wife asked at last.

"No—nothing at all!"

They are waiting for the Hansas—Per and Beret and their children—whose wagon broke down on the way to the homestead site. The Hansas arrive later, and the next day Per Hansa rides to Sioux Falls, fifty-two miles away, to file his claim. Meantime, Beret and the children set up housekeeping on the prairie, and Beret begins to wonder what the future holds for them in this lonely new land.

During the first day, both she and the boys found so much to do that they hardly took time to eat. They unloaded both wagons, set up the stove, and carried out the table. Then Beret arranged their bedroom in the larger wagon. With all the things taken out it was quite roomy in there; it made a tidy bedroom when everything had been put in order. The boys thought this work great fun, and she herself found some relief in it for her troubled mind. But something vague and intangible hovering in the air would not allow her to be wholly at ease; she had to stop often and look about, or stand erect and listen. . . . Was that a sound she heard? . . . All the while, the thought that had struck her yesterday when she had first got down from the wagon stood vividly before her mind: here there was nothing even to hide behind! . . . . When the room was finished, and a blanket had been hung up to serve as a door, she seemed a little less conscious of this feeling. But back in the recesses of her mind it still was there. . . .

After they had milked the cow, eaten their evening porridge, and talked awhile to the oxen, she took the boys and And-Ongen and strolled away from camp. With a common impulse, they went toward the hill; when they had reached the summit, Beret sat down and let her gaze wander aimlessly around. . . . In a certain sense, she had to admit to herself, it was lovely up here. The broad expanse stretching away endlessly in every direction, seemed almost like the ocean—especially now, when darkness was falling. It reminded her strongly of the sea, and yet it was very different.

. . . This formless prairie had no heart that beat, no waves that sang, no soul that could be touched . . . or cared. . . .

The infinitude surrounding her on every hand might not have been so oppressive, might even have brought her a measure of peace, if it had not been for the deep silence, which lay heavier here than in a church. Indeed, what was there to break it? She had passed beyond the outposts of civilization; the nearest dwelling places of men were far away. Here no warbling of birds rose on the air, no buzzing of insects sounded; even the wind had died away; the waving blades of grass that trembled to the faintest breath now stood erect and quiet, as if listening, in the great hush of the evening. . . . All along the way, coming out, she had noticed this strange thing: the stillness had grown deeper, the silence more depressing, the farther west they journeyed; it must have been over two weeks now since she had heard a bird sing! Had they travelled into some nameless, abandoned region? Could no living thing exist out here, in the empty, desolate, endless wastes of green and blue? . . . How *could* existence go on, she thought, desperately? If life is to thrive and endure, it must at least have something to hide behind!

What is homesteading? Why did the government offer it? Why did people accept the offer?

Settling Nebraska

Beret Hansa's feelings of unease about the prairie, which was so different from her native Norway, were similar to the feelings of Willa Cather, one of the best twentieth-century American novelists. Willa Cather was taken by her parents from Virginia to Nebraska in 1883 when she was nine. She came to love the prairie and in some of her fiction wrote memorable accounts of pioneer life in Nebraska.

Willa Cather Recalls Her Nebraska Childhood

In the following selection from a newspaper interview Willa Cather describes her reactions to Nebraska when she first moved there. For a fictional account of this same experience you may want to read her greatest novel, *My Antonia*.

My grandfather and grandmother had moved to Nebraska eight years before we left Virginia; they were among the real pioneers.

But it was still wild enough and bleak enough when we

got there. My grandfather's homestead was about eighteen miles from Red Cloud—a little town on the Burlington [Railroad], named after the old Indian chief who used to come hunting in that country, and who buried his daughter on the top of one of the river bluffs south of the town. Her grave had been looted for her rich furs and beadwork long before my family went West, but we children used to find arrowheads there and some of the bones of her pony that had been strangled above her grave. . . .

I shall never forget my introduction to it. We drove out from Red Cloud to my grandfather's homestead one day in April. I was sitting on the hay in the bottom of a Studebaker wagon, holding on to the side of the wagon box to steady myself—the roads were mostly faint trails over the bunch grass in those days. The land was open range and there was almost no fencing. As we drove further and further out into the country, I felt a good deal as if we had come to the end of everything—it was a kind of erasure of personality.

I would not know how much a child's life is bound up in the woods and hills and meadows around it, if I had not been jerked away from all these and thrown out into a country as bare as a piece of sheet iron. I had heard my father say you had to show grit in a new country, and I would have got on pretty well during that ride if it had not been for the larks. Every now and then one flew up and sang a few splendid notes and dropped down into the grass again. That reminded me of something—I don't know what, but my one purpose in life just then was not to cry, and every time they did it, I thought I should go under.

For the first week or two on the homestead I had that kind of contraction of the stomach which comes from homesickness. I didn't like canned things anyhow, and I made an agreement with myself that I would not eat much until I got back to Virginia and could get some fresh mutton. I think the first thing that interested me after I got to the homestead was a heavy hickory cane with a steel tip which my grandmother always carried with her when she went to the garden to kill rattlesnakes. She had killed a good many snakes with it, and that seemed to argue that life might not be so flat as it looked there.

We had very few American neighbors—they were mostly Swedes and Danes, Norwegians and Bohemians. I liked them from the first and they made up for what I missed in the country. I particularly liked the old women, they understood my homesickness and were kind to me. I had met 'traveled' people in Virginia and in Washington, but these old women on the farms were the first people who ever gave me the real feeling of an older world across the sea. Even when they spoke very little English, the old women somehow managed to tell me a great many stories about the old country. They talk more freely to a child than to grown people, and I always felt as if every word they said to me counted for twenty.

I have never found any intellectual excitement any more intense than I used to feel when I spent a morning with one of those old women at her baking or butter making. I used to ride home in the most unreasonable state of excitement; I always felt as if they told me so much more than they said—as if I had actually got inside another person's skin.

Why should people from Norway or Virginia feel so strange about settling on the prairie? What is there about this narrative that might lead you to believe that Willa Cather was destined to be a novelist?

The Land Rush in Oklahoma

The history of Oklahoma contains two of the most fascinating episodes in the westward movement. These were the land rushes of 1889 and 1893, when the government threw open several million acres of land to settlers on a first-come, first-served basis. The opening of these tracts in what had been set aside as Indian territory came at a time when choice land throughout the plains already had been taken up, and because the openings were well publicized throughout the country, the competition for farms and town lots was tremendous.

Hamilton Wicks Races to Guthrie

In the following report Hamilton Wicks describes the boom psychology and his own part in the race for free land in 1889. Unlike most of the "boomers," Wicks made the race by train. Guthrie, Oklahoma, where he claimed a town lot, was on the route of the Henry Ellsworth and Washington Irving expedition in 1832 (page 14).

And now the hour of twelve was at hand, and every one on the *qui vive* [alert] for the bugle blast that would dissolve the chain of enchantment hitherto girding about this coveted land. Many of the "boomers" were mounted on high-spirited and fleet-footed horses, and had ranged themselves along the territorial line, scarcely restrained even by the presence of the troops of cavalry from taking summary [immediate] possession. The better class of wagons and carriages ranged themselves in line with the horsemen, and even here and there mule teams attached to canvas-covered vehicles stood in the front ranks, with the reins and whip grasped by the "boomers" wives. All was excitement and expectation. Every nerve was on tension and every muscle strained.

Suddenly the air was pierced with the blast of a bugle. Hundreds of throats echoed the sound with shouts of exultation. The quivering limbs of saddled steeds, no longer restrained by the hands that held their bridles, bounded forward simultaneously into the "beautiful land" of Oklahoma; and wagons and carriages and buggies and prairie schooners and a whole congregation of curious equipages [carriages] joined in this unparalleled race, where every starter was bound to win a prize—the "Realization Stakes" of home and prosperity.

We, the spectators, witnessed the spectacle with most intense interest. Away dashed the thoroughbreds, the bronchos, the pintos, and the mustangs at a breakneck pace, across the uneven surface of the prairie. It was amazing to witness the recklessness of those cowboy riders. They jumped obstacles. They leaped ditches. They cantered with no diminution of speed through water-pools; and when they came to a ravine too wide to leap, down they would go with a rush, and up the other side with a spurt of energy, to scurry once more like mad over the level plain.

The occupants of our train now became absorbed in their own fate. . . . It was rather hard pulling for our engine until we reached the apex [top] of the Cimarron Valley, spread out in picturesque beauty at our very feet. Our train now rushed along the downgrade with the speed of a limited express crossing the fine bridge that spans the Cimarron with a roar, and swinging around the hills that intervened between the river and the Guthrie town site with the rapidity of a swallow's flight. All that there was of Guthrie, the now famous "magic city," on April 22, at 1:30 P.M., when the first train from the north drew up at the station and unloaded its first instalment of settlers, was a water-tank, a small station-house, a shanty for the Wells Fargo Express, and a Government Land Office.

I remember throwing my blankets out of the car window the instant the train stopped at the station. I remember tumbling after them through the self-same window. Then I joined the wild scramble for a town lot up the sloping hillside at a pace discounting any "go-as-you-please" race. There were several thousand people converging on the same plot of ground, each eager for a town lot which was to be acquired without cost and without price, each solely dependent on his own efforts, and animated by a spirit of fair play and good humor. The race was not over when you reached the particular lot you were content to select for your possession. The contest still was who should drive their stakes first, who would erect their tents soonest, and then, who would quickest build a little wooden shanty. It reminded me of playing blind-man's bluff. One did not know how far to go before stopping. It was hard to tell when it was best to stop; and it was a puzzle whether to turn to the right hand or the left.

I found myself, without exactly knowing why, about midway between the government building and depot [railroad station]. It occurred to me that a street would probably run past the depot. I accosted [approached] a man who looked like a deputy, with a piece of white card in his hands, and asked if this was to be a street along here.

"Yes," he replied. "We are laying off four corner lots right here for a lumber yard."

"Is this the corner where I stand?" I inquired.

"Yes," he responded, approaching me.

"Then I claim this corner lot!" I said with decision, as I jammed my location stick in the ground and hammered it securely home with my heel. . . .

An angry altercation [argument] ensued, but I stoutly maintained my position and my rights. I proceeded at once to unstrap a small folding-cot I brought with me, and by standing it on its end made a tolerable center-pole for a tent. I then threw a couple of my blankets over the pole, and staked them securely into the ground on either side. Thus I had a claim that was unjumpable [unbeatable] because of substantial improvements.

As night approached I strolled up on the eminence [high ground] near the land office, and surveyed the wonderful cyclorama spread out before me on all sides. Ten thousand people had "squatted" upon a square mile of virgin prairie that first afternoon, and as the myriad [multitude] of white tents suddenly appeared upon the face of the country, it was as though a vast flock of huge white-winged birds had just settled down upon the hillsides and in valleys. Here indeed was *a city laid out and populated in half a day*. Thousands of campfires sparkled upon the dark bosom of the prairie as far as the eye could reach.

I will never forget the first night of occupancy of this army. Unlike the hosts of the Assyrians that descended on the Israelites, their tents were not silent. On the contrary, there was a fusilade of shots on all sides from Winchesters, and Colts, and Remingtons, disturbing the stillness of the night, mingled with halloos, and shoutings, and the rebel yell, and the imitated warwhoop of the savage. I expected on the morrow to see the prairie strewn with gory corpses, but not a single corpse appeared, and I was not slow in making up my mind that nine-tenths of all the shots were fired in a mere wanton spirit of bravado [showing off] to intimidate a few such nervous tenderfeet as myself.

I was witness of all this magical municipal development, and could scarcely realize the miracle that was unfolding before me. The wealth-creating force that was displayed in the building up of Guthrie can not be better illustrated than in the fact that lots which had no value prior to April 22 sold in the center of the business district as high as five hundred dollars within a week thereafter, and a number changed hands before the expiration of the first month for one thousand, five hundred dollars each.

What is boom psychology? How is it revealed in this selection? in other selections in this booklet? What in addition to boom psychology accounts for the westward movement during the nineteenth century?

Index

1 2 3 4 5 6 7 8 9 10 FBFB 85 84 83 82 81 80 79 78 77 76